NEW SHOOTS
OLD TIPS
CAROLINE HOLMES

NEW SHOOTS
OLD TIPS

CAROLINE HOLMES

FRANCES LINCOLN

To David for the love we share in each other, our books and idiosyncrasies

Author's acknowledgements
My first huge thanks must go to Mukti Jain Campion, who listened to and guided my enthusiasm for garden voices from the past and coined the title *New Shoots, Old Tips*. Together we delved into garden writing to produce two BBC Radio Four series. This leads me to thank our interviewees: Peter Blackburn-Maze, Katie Butler, Graham Cox, Karen Kenny, Peter Jackson, Dr Robin Probert, Bob Sherman, Dr Sue Thompson, Michael Walker, Dr Twigs Way and, last but not least, my nephews James and Max. Loving thanks to my husband, David, narrator, book finder extraordinaire and provider of small trifles. Over twenty years ago Rosemary Nicholson of the Museum of Garden History fostered my researches into garden history and Philip Norman continues to be an incredibly helpful fount of knowledge. Many of the illustrations have come from the Museum's archives, for which many thanks. Thanks also to my audiences and many students who provide robust feedback and new grounds to forage. Thanks to Erica Hunningher for support and advice throughout; and finally to Jo Christian and Anne Askwith for tightening the threads of my weave of quotes and comments to produce this green tapestry.

Frances Lincoln Limited
4 Torriano Mews
Torriano Avenue
London NW5 2RZ

New Shoots, Old Tips
Copyright © Frances Lincoln 2004
Text copyright © Caroline Holmes 2004
Illustrations on pages 6, 24, 26, 29, 37, 39, 48, 52, 60 below, 61, 63, 64, 67, 78, 79, 93, 96, 97, 106, 119, 122, 125, 128, 131, 135, 148, 150, 151, 168 above, 172, 177 and 196 © Museum of Garden History. Illustration on page 165 by courtesy of the collection of the London Borough of Barnet
By arrangement with the BBC
The BBC logo is a trade mark of the British Broadcasting Corporation and is used under licence
BBC logo © BBC 1996
'New Shoots, Old Tips' is a Culture Wise production for BBC Radio 4

British Library Cataloguing-in-Publication data
A catalogue record for this book is available from the British Library
Printed and bound by Kyodo in Singapore
ISBN 0 7112 2367 X
9 8 7 6 5 4 3 2 1

Contents

Introduction

Gardening

Ever since people started gardening, there have been other people telling them how to do it better. Society has changed beyond recognition since, as the Book of Genesis tells us, 'the Lord God took the man, and put him into the Garden of Eden, to dress it, and to keep it', but the joys and disappointments that go hand in hand when working with weather, soil and plants are timeless. A hunt through old gardening writings is hugely enjoyable for, although the sentiments, experiences and cultural tips on gardening that writers have expressed over hundreds of years are at times arcane and zany, and accompanied by social mores that are in delicious contrast with those of today's gardening gurus, they mostly hold true across the centuries.

SUSTENANCE
The genesis of gardening was a gentle activity until Adam and Eve gave in to the temptation to taste the forbidden *tappauch*. Let us hope that they

A 1940s well-clothed rendition of Adam and Eve by the Tree of Knowledge beguiled by a decidedly active satanic serpent to the horror of a passing angel.

could still taste the sweet juices of that luscious fruit when they were cast out of the Garden of Eden, for thereafter they faced the rigours of subsistence gardening – 'Thorns also and thistles shall [the ground] bring forth to thee; and thou shalt eat the herb of the field; In the sweat of thy face shalt thou eat bread.' And so many a gardener has done ever since – for, as the Clown in Shakespeare's *Hamlet* comments, 'There is no ancient gentlemen but gardeners, ditchers and grave-makers: they hold up Adam's profession.'

Providing sustenance is one of the garden's prime functions – and in that sense George Bernard Shaw was right when he said in the twentieth century that 'Gardening is the only unquestionably useful job.' For many writers that role is a source of pleasure. For Thomas Hill, for instance, the greatest reward from gardening is 'that the same may furnish the owners and husbandmans table, with sundry seemely and dainty dishes to him of small cost'. Hill was an astrologer and jobbing writer who used the pseudonym Didymus Mountaine, and the author of *The Gardener's Labyrinth*, which was published in 1577, an extended version of his *Most Briefe and Pleasant Treatyse* of 1563 and *The Profitable Arte of Gardening* of 1571, the first book written for 'armchair gardeners'. His books combine garden gossip and a love of scented plants with practical plans and advice for modest gardens.

Thomas Jefferson, twice President of the United States of America, enjoyed the garden's productiveness. He kept a detailed *Garden and Farm Book* for his three Virginian estates. Whenever he was at Monticello, one of these estates, from 1776 to his death in 1824 he noted sowing, transplanting and harvesting times and a *Kalendar* of garden experiences. In 1811 he wrote to Charles Willson Peale:

Here … we are all farmers, but not in a pleasing style. We have so little labour in proportion to our land that, although perhaps we make more profit from the same labor, we cannot give to our grounds that style of beauty which satisfies the eye of the amateur … all are slovenly enough … I have often thought that if heaven had given me choice of my position and calling, it should have been on a rich spot of earth, well watered, and near a good market for the productions of the garden. No occupation is so delightful to me as the culture of the earth, and no culture comparable to that of the garden. Such a variety of subjects, some one always coming to perfection, the failure of one thing repaired by the success of another, and instead of one harvest a continued one through the year. Under a total want of demand except for our family table, I am still devoted to the garden. But though an old man, I am but a young gardener.

Just over fifty years after Jefferson's death, a gifted English artist and embroiderer and her mother bought a seemingly unpropitious site, Munstead Heath, in Surrey, overrun with bracken, and frequented by gypsies and occasional footpads and smugglers. The daughter, Gertrude Jekyll, went on in 1883 to create a celebrated garden across the road in 15 acres (6 hectares) of Munstead Wood, which inspired one of her many books, *Colour in the Flower Garden* (published in 1908 and in its third edition of 1914 retitled *Colour Schemes for the Flower Garden*), based on her experience at Munstead Wood and the garden design advice she had given to hundreds of clients. She too experienced the joys of garden harvest, writing sensually in that book:

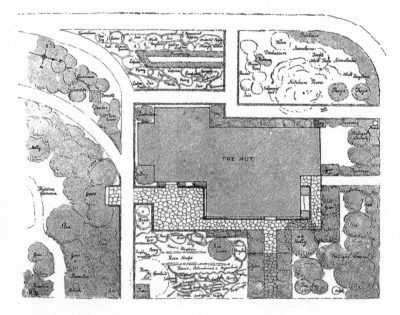

In 1894 Edwin Lutyens designed the Hut (not insubstantial) for Gertrude Jekyll, from which to work on her gardens. He followed this in 1897 with the house at Munstead Wood.

Surely my fruit garden would be not only a place of beauty, of pleasant sight and pleasant thought, but of leisurely repose, a repose broken only faintly and in welcome fashion by its own interests – in July, August and September a goodly place in which to wander and find luscious fruits in quantity that can be gathered and eaten straight from the tree. There is a pleasure in searching for and eating fruit in this way that is far better than having it picked by the gardener and brought in and set before one on a dish in a tame room. Is this feeling an echo of far-away days of savagery when men hunted for their food and rejoiced to find it, or is it rather the poet's delight of having direct intercourse with the good gift of the growing thing and seeing and feeling through all the senses how good and gracious the thing is? To pass the hand among the leaves of the Fig-tree, noting that they are a little harsh upon the upper surface and yet soft beneath; to be aware of their faint, dusky scent; to see the cracking of the coat of the fruit and the yellowing of the neck where it joins the branch – the two indications of ripeness – sometimes made clearer by the drop of honeyed moisture at the eye; then the handling of the fruit itself, which must needs be gentle because the tender coat is so readily bruised and torn; at the same time observing the slight greyish bloom and the colouring – low-toned transitions of purple and green; and finally to have the enjoyment of the luscious pulp, with the knowledge that it is one of the most wholesome and sustaining of fruit foods – surely all this is worthy garden service! Then how delicious are the sun-warmed Apricots and Peaches, and, later in the year, the Jargonelle Pears, always best eaten straight from the tree; and the ripe Mulberries of September. And how pleasant to stroll about the wide grassy ways, turning from the fruits to the flowers in the clumps and borders; to the splendid Yuccas and the masses of Hydrangea bloom, and then to the gorgeous Tritomas [now renamed Kniphofia] and other delights; and to see the dignity of the stately Bay-trees and the incomparable beauty of their every twig and leaf.

DELIGHT

Beauty has long been a purpose of the garden besides utility. In medieval times different terms indicated which role was more important in each area. Orchards are an excellent example: the word *pomerium* describes plantations for the serious production of fruit but the word *viridarium* describes fruit trees grown for blossom, shade and pleasure; in a medieval encyclopaedia Bartholomew de Glanville defines the *viridarium* as 'sometime ... yclept and ... a green place and merry with green trees and herbs'. *Hortus* or *ortus* was a general term for a garden but *gardinum* was effectively a kitchen garden, while the *herbarium* sported medicinal herbs and flowers planted around cut turf, designed for both delight and use.

The desire to share with readers their joy in the beauty of the garden is the concern of many writers, such as the American landscaper Andrew Jackson Downing. In the 1842 preface to his *Cottage Residences*, he writes: 'But I am still more anxious to inspire in the minds of my readers and countrymen more lively perceptions of the BEAUTIFUL in everything that relates to our houses and grounds. I wish to awaken a quicker sense of the grace, the elegance, or the picturesqueness of fine forms that are capable of being produced in these by Rural Architecture and Landscape Gardening – a sense will not only refine and elevate the mind, but pour into it new and infinite resources of delight.'

Jekyll also wrote, in *Wall and Water Gardens* (1901), of 'that simple human need for the solace of a quiet garden'. As well as being a place of beauty, the garden is a place where we can sit and indulge the senses – enjoying the view, running our hands through plants, nibbling a leaf, smelling a flower or listening to the birds. Perhaps as we seek to enjoy a garden in this way we should take a leaf out of Pliny's *Naturalis Historia* of the first century AD, an encyclopaedic work in thirty-seven volumes, containing myths, observation, cultivation advice and knowledge. In this work (in its Elizabethan translation by Philemon Holland) he describes how one man revelled in nature: 'There is a little hill named Carne within the territory of Tusculum ... clad with a goodly grove ... so even and round in the head, as if they were curiously kept, cut, and shorn artificially with garden shears ... In it there was one especial fair tree [which] ... Passenus Crispus, a man ... of great authority ... cast a fancy and extraordinary liking unto: insomuch as he was wont not only to take his repose and lie under it, to sprinkle and cast wine plentifully upon it, but also to clip, embrace, and kiss it otherwhiles.'

Pliny – Caius Plinius Secundus, better known as Pliny the Elder – was a well-travelled Roman official who held appointments in both the army and the navy. His tastes were sober by Roman standards and he loudly condemned evenings of raucous partying, much preferring the entertainment of poetry reading and music in a garden peristyle or courtyard. He maximized every hour of the day, for instance by being read to when being carried about the streets, sunbathing or in the bath. By studying other works and by observation, he tried to note every aspect of man and the world around him. *Naturalis Historia* remained a standard reference work throughout the medieval and Tudor periods. In the summer of AD 79 Pliny was admiral in command of the Roman fleet at Misenum in the Bay of Naples. He took a boat out to study a cloud of unusual size and appearance and the effects of the erupting Vesuvius. He stayed making copious notes until he was trapped and died. He would have been intrigued that the volcanic lava that engulfed Pompeii sealed invaluable evidence of first-century Roman gardens for today's archaeologists and historians.

William Coles devotes a chapter to the 'Joys of a Garden' in his *Art of Simpling* of 1656:

As for recreation, if a man be wearied with over-much study (for study is a wearinesse to the Flesh as Solomon by experience can tell you) there is no better place in the world to recreate himself than a Garden, there being no sence but may be delighted therein.

If his sight be obfuscated and dull, as it may easily be, with continually poring, there is no better way to relieve it, than to view the pleasant greenesse of Herbes, which is the way that Painters use, when they have almost spent their sight by their most earnest contemplation of brighter objects: neither doe they only feed the Eyes, but comfort the wearied Braine with fragrant smells which yield a certaine kind of nourishment.

The Eares also (which are called the Daughters of Musick, because they delight therein) have their recreation by the pleasant noise of the warbling notes, which the chaunting birds accent forth from amongst the murmuring Leaves.

As for the Taste, they serve it so exceedingly, that whether it be affected with sweet, sower, or bitter things, they even prostitute themselves. And for the feeling likewise they entertain it with as great variety as can be imagined, there being some plants as soft as silke, and some as prickly as an Hedgehogge; so that there is no outward sense which can want satisfaction in this Cornucopia. And if the outward senses be so delighted, the inward will be so too, it being as it were the School of Memory and Fancy … A house though otherwise beautifull, yet if it hath no Garden belonging to it, is more like a Prison than a House.

Thomas Hill was greatly in favour of a 'Garden of pleasure and delight'. He writes:

The life of man in this world is but a thraldom, when the Sences are not pleased; and what rarer object can there be on earth, (the motions of the Celestial bodies excepted) then a beautifull and Odoriferous Garden plat Artifically composed, where he may read and contemplate on the wonderfull works of the great Creator, in Plans and Flowers; for if he observeth with a judicial eye, and a serious judgement their variety of Colours, Sents, Beauty, Shapes, Interlacing, Enamiling, Mixture, Turnings, Windings, Embosments, Operations and Vertues, it is most admirable to behold, and meditate upon the same. But now to my Garden of flowers and sweet Hearbs.

Albert, Count of Bollstadt, aka Albertus Magnus, was born *c.* 1206 at Lauingen in Swabia, studied in Padua and entered the Dominican order. His legacy to gardening was a treatise, *On Vegetables and Plants*, which provides practical and aesthetic guidance, and in which he extols the garden's simple savours:

Care must be taken that the lawn is of such a size that about it in a square may be planted every sweet-smelling herb such as rue, and sage and basil, and likewise all sorts of flowers, as the violet, columbine lily, rose, iris and the like. So that between these herbs and the turf, at the edge of the lawn set square, let there be a higher bench of turf flowering and lovely: and somewhere in the middle provide seats so that men may sit down there to take their repose pleasurably when their senses need refreshment … The pleasure garden needs to have a free current of air along with shade. It also needs to be considered that the trees should not be bitter ones whose shade gives rise to diseases, such as the walnut and some others: but let them be sweet trees, with perfumed flowers and agreeable shade, like grapevines, pears, apples, pomegranates, sweet bay trees, cypresses and such like.

Behind the lawn there may be great diversity of medicinal and scented herbs, not only to delight the sense of smell by their perfume but to refresh the sight with the variety of their flowers, and to cause admiration at their many forms in those who look at them.

TOIL

Although writers capture the sensual joy of a garden they are well aware of the sweat in gardening. The mantra of many ancient texts seems to be that diligence leads to reward mostly by toil: get out and sweat a little, rejoice in desirable seedlings and destroy the thugs as you weed and dig. Some Roman writers advocate gentle tending – advice echoed occasionally by eighteenth-century landscapers and Arts and Crafts gardeners. Most consider constant work – clearing up every stray leaf, regular trimming of dead flower heads, removal of molehills and so on – to be the essence of the joy of gardening.

Pliny expresses the need to toil when he writes about a freed slave whose neighbours jealously accused him of witchcraft because his small ground was so fruitful. The slave defends himself: ' "My masters, behold! These are the sorceries, charms, and all the enchantments that I use (pointing to his daughter, his oxen, and furniture). I might besides allege mine own travail and toil that I take, the early rising and late sitting up, the careful watching and the painful sweats which I daily endure." By which example verily, a man may soon see, that good husbandry goeth not all by much expense: but it is painstaking and careful diligence that doth the deed.' Pliny also records that the daughter was 'a lusty strong lass and big of bone … well fed, and as well clad', making the point – echoed by Jefferson, Jekyll and a host of other garden writers – that successful gardeners eat better and enjoy good health.

Like the slave, Thomas Hill argues for diligence: 'The husbandman or Gardener shall enjoy a most commodious and delectable Garden … not sufficient is it to a Gardener, that he knoweth, or would the furtherance of the Garden, without any cost bestowed, which the works and labours of the same require; nor the will againe of the workman, in doing and bestowing of charges, shall smally availe without he have both art and skill in the same … to understand and know what to begin and follow.' For him the key to success is not only labour but also knowledge and skill.

William Lawson was a clergyman who received the order of deacon at Durham and then became vicar of Hutton Ruby. In 1618 he published

A New Orchard and Garden, based on forty-eight years' experience of gardening in the north – an historic reference book for gardeners with colder gardens and a touch of moral rectitude, in which he writes: 'Your gardiner had not need to be an idle or lazie lubber.'

His stern words contrast with Rudyard Kipling's more light-hearted lines from 'The Glory of the Garden' of 1911 –

> Oh, Adam was a gardener, and God who made him sees
> That half a proper gardener's work is done upon his knees,
> So when your work is finished, you can wash your hands and pray
> For the Glory of the Garden, that it may not pass away!
> And the Glory of the Garden it shall never pass away!

– and Jekyll's more elegantly contemporary sentiments expressed in an article entitled 'The Mixed Border': 'There is no day in the blooming life of the late summer border, or indeed of any other, when it does not need close watching and some kind of tending. Many people think that to have a good border of summer flowers is an easy thing; whereas to have it well done so as to show a continual picture of plant beauty, even for three months, is one of the most difficult of horticultural feats.'

Charles Dudley Warner gave practical and gung-ho advice, sensibly suggesting, 'What a man needs in gardening is a cast-iron back, with a hinge in it.' In 1918 he published a compilation of garden writings, including his own 'My Summer in a Garden', which displays a more luxurious approach to gardening:

What is a garden for? The pleasure of man. I should take much more pleasure in a shady garden. Am I to be sacrificed, broiled, roasted, for the sake of the increased vigour of a few vegetables? The thing is perfectly absurd. If I were rich I think I would have my garden covered with an awning, so that it would be comfortable to work in it. It might roll up and be removable as the great awning of the Coliseum was – not like the Boston one which went off in a high wind. Another very good way to do, and probably not so expensive as the awning, would be to have four persons ... carry a sort of canopy over you as you hoed. And there might be a person at each end of the row with some cool refreshing drink. Agriculture is still at a very barbarous stage. I hope to live yet to see the day when I can do my gardening, as tragedy is done, to slow and soothing music, and attended by some of the comforts I have named. These things come so forcibly into my wind sometimes as I work, that perhaps, when a wandering breeze lifts my straw hat, or a bird lights on a near currant-bush, and shakes out a full-throated summer song, I almost expect to find the cooling drink and the hospitable entertainments at the end of the row. But I never do. There is nothing to be done but to turn round and hoe back to the other end.

But for all the toil the gardener will be rewarded. That is the theme of many a writer, such as the monk Walafrid Strabo, who, in a delightful Latin poem, *Hortulus*, of about 840 AD writes: 'If you do not refuse to harden or dirty your hands ... to spread whole baskets of dung on the sun-parched soil – then, you may rest assured, your soil will not fail you.'

Labour in the garden can provide refreshment from other activities, according to the seventeenth-century philosopher John Locke: 'The great men among the ancients understood very well how to reconcile manual labour with affairs of state, and thought it no lessening to their dignity to make the one the recreation to the other. That indeed which seems most generally to have employed and diverted their spare hours, was agriculture. Gideon among the Jews was taken from threshing, as well as Cincinnatus amongst the Romans from the plough, to command the armies of their countries ... and, as I remember, Cyrus thought gardening so little beneath the dignity and grandeur of a throne, that he showed Xenophon a large field of fruit trees all of his own planting ... Delving, planting, inoculating, or any the like profitable employments would be no less a diversion than any of the idle sports in fashion, if men could be brought to delight in them.' Writers echo his sentiments through the nineteenth century and beyond.

Moral virtue is another benefit. Generations of garden writers have extolled the virtues of being at one with your soil. Samuel Reynolds Hole, later Dean of Rochester and rose authority, had gardened as a child with his sisters at Caunton Manor near Newark in the 1820s. In *Our Gardens* (1899) he writes wisely: 'The principal value in a private garden is not understood. It is not to give the possessor vegetables and fruit (that can be better and cheaper done by the market-gardeners), but to teach him patience and philosophy, and the higher virtues – hope deferred, and expectations blighted, leading directly to resignation, and sometimes to alienation.'

Perhaps it was the association between virtue and gardening that prompted John Claudius Loudon to write: 'We can hardly conceive any rural pursuits more adapted for a clergyman than natural history and gardening.' John Claudius Loudon was a Lanarkshire farmer's son who at the age of sixteen was apprenticed as draughtsman and hothouse assistant to John Mawer, an Edinburgh landscape gardener and nurseryman. He then went to live and work with another nurseryman, Mr Dickson, and in his spare time attended classes at Edinburgh University in drawing, arithmetic, botany and chemistry, adding agriculture later. He travelled to London in 1803 and published an *Encyclopaedia of Gardening* in 1822, which remained the standard horticultural manual throughout the nineteenth century and is an accurate reference book in the twenty-first. In 1826 he founded the *Gardener's Magazine*, based in an office in his Bayswater villa, in which he was greatly assisted by his wife Jane, who continued the good work after his death in 1843. Through its quarterly, then bimonthly and then monthly columns, Loudon reached a wide range of gardeners and cottagers, and hoped 'to put them on a footing with those about the metropolis'. Zealous and immensely productive, he wrote many other meticulous gardening books including the *Encyclopaedia of Cottage, Farm and Villa Architecture and Furniture* (1833) with 1,150 pages, which Jane transcribed by hand, and *The Villa Gardener* (1850).

NATURE AS ART
Gardening writers share an awareness of all aspects of the natural world and their relevance to their gardening success.

Today we may not have the knowledge of astronomy demanded by Virgil, quoted by Thomas Hill as saying, 'A husbandman should be skilful in the winds, and have the foreknowledge and predictions of them: also to have an insight in the nature and influence of the stars.' Nor may we respond to the considerable amount of advice available regarding planting by the phases of the moon, such as that of Thomas Tusser. Tusser farmed (unsuccessfully) at Cattiwade and Brantham in Suffolk and West Dereham in Norfolk. In 1557 he published a hundred points of good husbandry, followed by *Five Hundred Points of Good Husbandry* in 1573, a month-by-month calendar of operations, written in doggerel. His advice is good, the doggerel delightful, but sadly he died in penury before his books became best-sellers. He writes:

> Cut all thing or gather, the Moone in the wane,
> but soe in encreasing, or give it his bane.

In simple terms the moon draws out and up, so sow your seeds as the moon is waxing but harvest when it is in the wane. Advice today is much the same except leaf crops are separated from roots: sow and harvest leaves when the moon is waxing and roots when it is waning.

But generally writers' observations are pertinent to us today. For instance, in *The Villa Gardener* Loudon remarks: 'An irregular surface is always attended by an irregular climate. This is occasioned by the "different" influence of the sun on surfaces of different degrees of slope; and by the different degrees of interruption which hills or irregularities of different shapes and sizes give to the wind' – sentiments that will be shared especially by colder-zone gardeners, who have to guard against frost pockets.

Loudon's fellow Scot Philip Miller writes in his *Gardener's Dictionary* (first published in 1731): 'In short, a Garden necessarily requires the Sun, a good Soil, the Care of the Gardener, and Water; and the last, above all, is indispensably necessary: without of these there's no Good to be expected: and it would be egregious Folly to plant a Garden where any of these are wanting.' Miller was one of many expatriate Scots gardeners in the eighteenth century, of whom English garden designer Stephen Switzer (of serpentine path fame) acidly wrote, 'by the help of a little learning and a great deal of Impudence, they invade these Southern Provinces'. Miller was an observant gardener for fifty years to the Worshipful Company of Apothecaries and director of their Chelsea Physic Garden from 1722. He actively favoured his countrymen who shared the Scottish Puritan work ethic, frugality and a good education. *The Gardener's Dictionary*, which went into eight editions and six abridgements, incorporated the then new Linnaean binomial nomenclature, covering plants alphabetically from Abele tree to Ziziphus.

Thomas Tusser captures the seasonal nature of gardening:

> At spring (for the sommer) sowe garden ye shall,
> at harvest (for winter) or sowe not at all.
> Oft digging, removing, and weeding (ye see),
> makes herbe the more holesome and greater to bee.

Frontispiece.

> Time fair, to sowe or to gather be bold,
> but set or remoove when the weather is cold.

The earlier the advice the more geographically focused it was, so the relevance of the advice may depend on the locality of the writer's garden. Tusser for instance reckons of spring winds:

> The north is a noyer to grasse of all suites,
> The east a destroyer to herbe and all fruites:
> The south with his showers refresheth the corne,
> The west to all flowers may not be forborne.

As a fellow East Anglian I can vouch for the fact that the easterly winds that come from Siberia and northerly from the Arctic Circle both rapidly ruin our spring weather and damage the green blade as it riseth.

THE BENEFITS OF LEARNING

That we can all learn about gardening is the tenor of the words of many writers. Ralph Austen preaches the benefits of experience, saying philosophically in *The Spiritual Use of an Orchard* (published with *A Treatise of Fruit Trees* in 1653), 'Experience is called the Perfecter of Arts, and most sure, and best teacher in any Arts. Contemplation and Action are the two Leggs whereon Arts runne stedily and strongly, and the one without the other can but hop, or go lonely.'

John Evelyn in *The Compleat Gard'ner* (1693) believes that the landed gentry should do some reading:

How necessary it is for a Gentleman, who designs to have Fruit and Kitchen-Gardens, to be at least reasonably Instructed in what relates to those kind of Gardens.

The most Considerable of those Pleasures, is not only to be able to obtain what may be produced by Earth, that shall have been well ordered, and a Ground well improv'd with Trees that perhaps shall have been Graffed, Planted, Prun'd, Cultivated, etc., by ourselves,

There is nothing 'mean' or 'pitiful' in Miller's frontispiece design (see page 26) and the heavens seem ready to rain a cornucopia of fresh bounty.

though really the Ideas of such Injoyments are powerful Charms to engage us to the Study of them.

Thinking of those at the other end of the social scale, Sam Beeton, husband of Mrs Beeton of *The Book of Household Management* fame, opens his *Shilling Gardening Book* of the 1860s with the words: 'The love of gardening among Englishmen and Scotchmen, too, is steadily on the increase, and has been so for a long series of years; and therefore the demand for such handbooks as these in which gardening as it ought to be done is described briefly but tersely, and in a manner which the lowest capacity ought to be able to grasp and assimilate.'

J.C. Loudon's wife Jane wrote extensively in her own right. While J.C. Loudon's writing is constrained by his dour Scottish upbringing, Jane's writing in *The Amateur Gardener* (1847) although dated, makes lighter and more enjoyable reading. In this extract she wryly reminds readers to learn from others:

Shut your own Gate behind you
When you leave your garden, fruit patch, or grounds, of whatever kind, shut the gate, and leave whatever is behind it there – don't take it with you. Recollect that when you visit the place of another, you go to see what he has to show and learn what he has to teach. If you would be a welcome visitor, and be dismissed with a pressing invitation to come again, place yourself in a receptive mood; be for the time the attentive pupil and not the teacher. When others visit your place, will be the proper time to teach. Of all the intolerable bores who visit us is the man who brings his own place with him, and who, whatever may be shown him, at once institutes a comparison with his own, and begins to tell that 'mine are much better than that' – 'I can beat you on so and so,' and ignoring the thing before him tells us 'Ah you should see my strawberries', 'my roses', 'my tomatoes' and so on all through – in short the man who does not 'shut his own gate behind him'. Those who are so thoroughly satisfied with their own that they cannot forget it for a few hours, should not visit, but remain upon the scene of their remarkable achievements – at home. We would not imply that one in visiting the grounds of another, may not, on occasion, drop a useful hint drawn from his own experience, that he

may not give his host any information that he may ask for. But we have been so annoyed at receiving visitors, and worse still, in visiting strange grounds in company with those whose only object in visiting appears to be to boast of their own affairs, that we feel called upon to protest against it. Those who thoughtlessly fall into this unpleasant error, need only to be reminded of it, and they will sensibly avoid it. From the chronic boaster of his own achievements, we hope to be delivered.

Heeding Jane Loudon's words, we gardeners today can learn what writers of the past have to teach about gardening. I hope that from their old tips gathered in this book you will find plenty of new shoots of useful information to apply to your own gardens.

Gardeners

WOMEN

Early writers assume that a man is in charge of the garden, does the heavy work and produces vegetables (as did my late Suffolk neighbour, who once leaned on our fence and confided that vegetables are not a woman's job). However Roman garden writer M. Terentius Varro wrote a manual entitled *Rerum rusticarum* for his prospective widow in 36 BC (a year before his death) on agriculture, horticulture and managing his properties including the ancestral demesne at Reate (Rieti), a luxurious farm at Casinium (Cassino) and villas at Tusculum and Cumae.

Varro obviously had not read about the deleterious effect of menstruating women. According to Democritus, whom Pliny repeats, a woman 'who first obeys her youth's fixed laws, barefooted and ashamed [in the throes of first menstruation] should be led three times around the flowerbeds, when any caterpillars will instantly fall and die'. Many gardeners would count such an effect as a blessing – but not the next effect Pliny describes: '… the herbs and young buds in a garden if they do but pass by, will catch a blast, and burn away to nothing. Sit they upon or under trees while they are in this case, the fruit which hangeth upon them will fall.' Maybe these beliefs protected women from the labours of gardening once a month.

Guiding the husbandman and his family to bountiful harvests from farm and garden, Thomas Tusser writes:

> The husband is he that to labour doth fall,
> the labour of him I doe husbandrie call.

Most vegetables were grown on a field scale, whereas the garden of pot herbs, herbs, simples and flowers was the woman's domain, her kingdom an expression of her successful home rule. Tusser continues:

> In March and in April, from morning to night,
> in sowing and setting, good huswives delight:
> To have in a garden, or other like plot,
> to turn up their house, and to furnish their pot.

That delight would be success, at a time when there was little control over feast and famine, from the bounty of a well-tended garden that provided visual and culinary pleasure. Hence the saying 'Where Rosemary flourishes the lady rules'. Rosemary, which can be difficult to grow, was an essential, indeed life-saving herb. Ensuring it flourished year round guaranteed a regular supply for food and medicine (not to mention a hair rinse with mild insecticidal properties).

Many writers, however, expect women to confine their efforts to growing flowers – as Andrew Downing does in *Cottage Residences* (1842):

> The master of the premises we shall suppose capable of managing the kitchen garden, the fruit trees, the grass, and the whole of the walks, himself, with perhaps the assistance of a common gardener, or labouring man, for a day or two, at certain seasons of the year. The mistress and her daughter, or daughters, we shall suppose to have sufficient fondness for flowers, to be willing and glad to spend three times a week, an hour or two, in the cool mornings and evenings of summer, in the pleasing task of planting, tying to neat stakes, picking off decayed flowers, and removing weeds from the borders, and all other operations that so limited a garden may require.

William Lawson understood how important it is to gain confidence with just a small selection of easy plants such as herbs. Despite his patronizing tone beginning gardeners could do worse than follow his strictures in *The Country House-Wifes Garden* (1623): 'I recken these hearbes onely, because I teach my Country Housewife, not skilful Artists ... Let her first grow cunning in this, and then she may inlarge her garden, as her skill and ability increaseth.' I would apply the advice to men and children as well.

In *Practical Instructions in Gardening for Ladies*, published in 1840, Jane Loudon advises: 'Whatever doubts may be entertained as to the practicability of a lady attending to the culture of culinary vegetables and fruit trees, none can exist respecting her management of the flower garden. That is pre-eminently a woman's department. The culture of flowers implies the lightest possible kind of garden labour.'

CHILDREN

Roman illustrations show children studying in gardens while their poorer contemporaries scared birds, collected stones and undertook a host of other menial agricultural and horticultural tasks. That balance was evident in the nineteenth century, when gardening became a suitable outdoor activity for young of the better sort.

The young William Cobbett spent lonely days as a bird scarer and stone picker, his father having been reduced to being a day labourer. Cobbett grew up to become a radical reformer and pamphleteer in England and the United States. He wrote *A Cottage Economy* in 1823 for the rural poor and in 1829 the lengthily titled *The English Gardener, or, A Treatise On the Situation, Soil, Enclosing and Laying-out, of Kitchen Gardens; on the Making and Managing of Hot-beds and Green-Houses; and on the Propagation and Cultivation of all sorts of Kitchen-Garden Plants, and of Fruit-Trees whether of the Garden or the Orchard.* In *A Cottage Economy* he promotes the idea of children gardening: 'Children observe and follow their parents in almost everything. How much better, during a long and dreary winter, for daughters, and even sons, to assist, or attend, their mother, in a green-house, than to be seated with her at cards, or in the blubberings over a stupid novel, or any other amusement that can possibly be conceived.'

Although his language is outmoded, J.C. Loudon reminds me of the joy I felt as a child when I had my small watering can and, even better, was let loose with a hose – a joy my children later shared and now my nephews – when he writes in *The Suburban Gardener and Villa Companion* (1838):

What pleasure have not children in applying their little green watering-pans to plants in pots, or pouring water in at the roots of favourite

A wife and her dog, armed with essential rake, spade, fork and watering can, defy you to offer anything other than praise for their abundantly productive plot.

flowers in borders? And what can be more rational than the satisfaction which the grown up amateur, or master of the house, enjoys, when he returns from the city to his garden in the summer evenings, and applies the syringe to his wall trees, with refreshing enjoyment to himself and the plants, and to the delight of his children, who may be watching his operations? ... What more delightful than to see the master or mistress of a small garden or pleasure-ground, with all the boys and girls, the maids, and, in short, all the strength of the house, carrying pots and pails of water to different parts of the garden; and to see the refreshment produced to the soil and plants by the application of the watering pan and the syringe?

There are many ways in which gardening can be made enjoyable for children. For instance, Bunny Guinness in her *Family Gardens* (1996) shows readers how to create a selection of water and child-friendly ideas that flow seamlessly into a garden's overall design. Jane Taylor has created a Monet's garden with a difference at the 4H Children's Garden at Michigan State University. Large bronze frogs decorate lily pads and on the pool edge are two swing bars for children which make the frogs draw up water and spit out a drenching arch across the pool.

Queen Victoria and Prince Albert encouraged their nine children to garden around Swiss Cottage in the grounds of Osborne House on the Isle of Wight. Each child had a set of monogrammed tools and fourteen rectangular beds in which to produce fruit, vegetables and flowers for the main house. They kept account books, buying in seed and selling their produce to the kitchens – seeming to a modern parent to be terrifyingly and uncharacteristically well ordered. Alicia Amherst, who wrote one of the first books on garden history, describes and praises the royal children's gardens in a later book, *Children's Gardens* (1907), written under her married name the Honourable Mrs Evelyn Cecil (and reading like a practical version of Frances Hodgson Burnett's *The Secret Garden*). She also urges parents to encourage young gardeners, providing design and seasonal ideas for them: 'Children do not often have the choice of a garden. They must, as a rule take what is given them and make the best of it. But once the ground is assigned to them, much can be done to make it pretty, attractive, and original ... I wonder if you know the fairy-tale which tells how if a tulip is kissed when open in the sunshine a tiny fairy will come out of it?' Fairy

A postcard dated 21 August 1925 shows the gardening implements, all individually monogrammed, used by the nine children of Victoria and Albert at Osborne House on the Isle of Wight.

gardens were a popular Victorian and Edwardian conceit.

Ethelind Fearon perpetuates the idea of the worthiness of children gardening in *The Young Market Gardeners* (1953). Her Blytonesque characters – 'There were six of us: me and my friend Gordon Rivers who was then fifteen; Richard and Jimmy Adams and their sister Clara, who is a decent sort of girl and very strong for digging but does not get in the way; Gordon's sister Mary who is no good for anything except doing what she is told' – raise all sorts of commercial crops (without the aid of lashings of ginger beer), offering enthusiastic advice throughout.

RICH EXTRAVAGANCE

From the seventeenth century onwards, armed with the instructions of increasing numbers of gardening tomes, the middle classes created gardens inspired by the great gardens of the landed gentry.

But how to decant their grand designs with a confident leap into pint pots? As Philip Miller rightly observes: 'In the Business of Designs a mean and pitiful Manner ought to be studiously avoided, and the Aim should always be at that which is great and noble; not to make Cabinets and Mazes small, and Basons like Bowldishes, and Alleys so narrow, that two Persons can scarce walk in them. It is much better to have but two or three Things pretty large, than four times the Number of small ones, which are but Trifles. Before the Design of a Garden be put in Execution, it ought to be considered what it will be in twenty or thirty Years time ...'

There were many for whom designing in 'a mean and pitiful manner' was no problem. Anthony a Wood chronicled Oxford University life in the years leading up to the Civil War (and is quoted in Eleanour Sinclair Rohde's *Oxford College Gardens*, 1932). He moaned about the extravagance of Sir Thomas Clayton, Warden of Merton: '... new trees planted, arbours made, rootes of choice flowers bought etc. All which tho unnecessary, yet the poore college must pay for them and all this to please a woman. Not content with these matters, there must be a new summer-house built at the south end of the warden's garden, wherein her ladyship and her gossips may take their pleasure ... And this the warden told the society that it would not cost the college above £20 yet when it was finished there was £100 paid for it by the bursar, wanting some few shillings.'

When Queen Caroline, consort of George II, died in 1737 she left a debt of £12,000 as a result of her extravagant gardening at Richmond Gardens, which later became the Royal Botanic Gardens at Kew.

Amongst the richest Victorian and Edwardian gardeners were the Rothschild family. One of their gardeners, Ernest Field, observed wryly: 'Rich people used to show their wealth by the size of their bedding plant list; 10,000 for a squire, 20,000 for a baronet, 30,000 for an earl and 40,000 for a duke.' One year at the dawn of the twentieth century, 50,000 plants were used for the parterre at Waddesdon Manor. The *Bucks Herald* on 3 July 1889 reported on Waddesdon Manor: 'Less than 15 years ago ... the

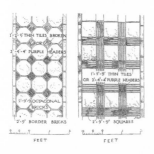 

LEFT *In* Gardens for Small Country Houses *(1932) Gertrude Jekyll provided drawings and descriptions of mixed paving. She favoured local materials and her 'thin tiles' make an ideal non-slip surface.* RIGHT *Two of Thomas Bewick's quadrapeds in characteristic mode.*

beautiful site now crowned with a house which looks like a historic French chateau, was purely pastoral land. Farms have been swept away, cornfields have been transformed into flower gardens, trees brought from immense distances have been transplanted, with a success that tells of a new era in English forestry, and out of a tangled wilderness has, by process of determined cultivation, arisen a Park and Estate probably unequalled in England.' A railway was built to transport the materials to the virgin site. Maintaining the gardens to the 'Waddesdon standard' included replanting the parterre overnight when the blooms were destroyed by storms. Another of the Rothschild properties – which included Gunnersbury Park, where the Japanese Ambassador remarked about the Japanese Garden, 'We have nothing like this in Japan' – was Exbury, where, on 260 acres (105 hectares), Lionel Rothschild II planted 1,000,000 rhododendrons and camellias, and employed 150 men for 10 years to build 22 miles of irrigation pipes. The gardens were staffed by 20 senior gardeners and 100 under gardeners.

Big houses could afford stylish horticultural extravagances. When these went out of fashion they would be discarded and the head gardener would disperse them amongst his friends and neighbours in the village. How true today are the sentiments Mrs Loftie expressed in 1879 in *Social Twitters*:

> It is often amusing to trace a fashion as it percolates downwards. By the time it has reached the far-away sleepy country villages something quite new and entirely opposite is really the rage amongst the upper ten thousand. Cottagers now try to fill their little plots with geraniums and calceolarias, which they are obliged to keep indoors at great inconvenience to themselves and loss of light to their rooms. Meantime my lady at the Court is hunting the nursery grounds for London Pride and gentianella to make edgings in her wilderness, and for the fair tall rockets, the cabbage roses, and nodding columbines which her pensioners have discarded and thrown away.

A NEED FOR THRIFT

Shirley Hibberd argues in his splendidly named *Rustic Adornments for Homes of Taste* of 1856 that

> ... the Home of Taste is not necessarily the result of a lavish expenditure – the most humble may command it. Though the several

This delightfully informal portrait of father, son, daughter and family pets relaxing in their fashionable 'rustic' seat is captioned 'Knoll Cottage 1909'.

Rustic Adornments treated of in this work admit of extension, commensurate with the most liberal outlay, there is not one but is in some measure attainable by those who have but little leisure and most narrow means, and indeed may be, and have been cultivated most successfully by those who could not aspire even to the ordinary luxuries of middle life ... He who lays out his garden in accordance with correct principles of taste, may find in it as much amusement, and as genuine a solace from the cark and care of life, as if it were a domain of thousands of acres – perhaps more so, for it is his own work, it represents his own idea, it is a part of himself, and hence redolent of heart-ease.

But for many country gardeners, from before Tusser's time when *The Ladder to Thrift* was

> To get good plot to occupie,
> and store and use it husbandlie,

right up to the 1960s, gardening was primarily about growing vegetables and fruit for survival.

William Cobbett wrote *Cottage Economy* to instruct families living at subsistence level in thrifty ways that would improve their lives and their diets. He did so in a tone that courts no discussion: 'And is it not much more rational for parents to be employed in teaching their children how to cultivate a garden ... to make bread, beer, bacon, butter, and cheese, and to be able to do these things for themselves, or for others, than to leave them to prowl about the lanes and commons or to mope at the heels of some crafty, sleek-headed pretended saint, who while he extracts the last penny from their pockets, bids them be contented with their misery.'

The book is liberally sprinkled with political and social comment. Here is an example: '... it is the custom to allot to labourers "a potatoe ground" in part-payment of their wages! This has a tendency to bring English labourers down to the state of the Irish, whose mode of living, as to food, is but one remove from that of the pig, and of the ill-fed pig too ... An acre of land, that will produce 300 bushels of potatoes, will produce 32 bushels of wheat ... the raw potatoes will yield 1,830 lb of nutritious matter ... wheat ... yields 2,080 of bread.' His calculations are based on peeling the potatoes.

The following thrifty 'tip' from him is typical: 'Mustard Why buy this, when you can grow it in your garden? The stuff you buy is half drugs, and is injurious to health. A yard square of ground, sown with common Mustard, the crop of which you would grind for use, in a little mustard-mill, as you wanted it, would save you some money, and probably save your life. Your mustard would look brown instead of yellow; but the former colour is as good as the latter: and, as to the taste, the real mustard

According to Sam Beeton, broken flowerpots could be utilized for shading vulnerable plants.

has certainly a much better than that of the drugs and flour, which go under the name of mustard.'

From the nineteenth century onwards, writers have imparted plenty of advice to the not so well-to-do on Doing It Yourself. The anonymous author of *A New System of Practical Domestic Economy* (1825), for instance, who advises: 'One final point of economy we shall recommend is, to avoid as much as possible all artificial ornaments in small gardens, unless we wish for a floral toy-shop. These things are always in bad taste, either with regard to selection or size.'

Marion Cran, too, encourages readers to do things themselves. Between 1910 and 1941 Cran recorded her experiences of gardening at Coggers in Surrey and her travels through Canada, the United States, Africa, Europe and Australia, where she visited gardens and observed them from train windows, and these writings were collected in *Garden Wisdom*. She describes her garden in toe-curling fashion: 'If I had found a garden made of another dreamer's labour it would never have been so truly mine as that beggar-maid, that ragged waif of the hills which went royally decked in the jewels I toiled for and won for her out of the treasure chest of the Old Mother.' Her essays include suggestions such as: 'Steps are easy to construct. They cost a good deal if workmen and architects are engaged for the purpose; but if they are done in odd moments they need cost little more than those rare and precious things which we spend so niggardly in life – thought and energy.' If you take her advice, I suggest spending thought and energy in careful planning, too, so as not to create a potential death trap in the garden.

Gardeners in the past made the best of what surrounded them, going into the woods and hedgerows to get sticks from hazel and other trees to use as bean poles and plant supports, or honeysuckle to bind. The Latin genus name for privet, *Ligustrum*,

A high-class adjustable ladder, new-fangled secateurs and a panama hat allowed a gentleman to perfect his rose display.

comes from *ligare*, meaning to tie up or bind; the plant was used by Pliny, who recommended tying up plants with its flexy withies.

Use what grows locally and naturally, advises Reginald Blomfield in *The Formal Garden in England* (1892): '... the guelder rose grows wild in the meadow and the spindle-tree in the wood, and the rowan, the elder, and the white-thorn; and the wild cherry in autumn fires the woodland with its crimson and gold. Every one admires these as a matter of proper sensibility to nature, but it does not seem to occur to people that they would grow with as little difficulty in a garden, and at the very smallest expense. It would undoubtedly injure the business of the nursery gardener to allow that they were possible.' The approach was for once one that Blomfield's arch enemy William Robinson – who in *The English Flower Garden* (1883) and many other writings argued for informality in garden design – ought to have approved. Although now when we want new plants we can pop out to a nursery or garden centre, it is certainly worth noting what thrives in neighbouring gardens before making your shopping list. But rather than buying plants, try sharing and swapping cuttings and seeds with other enthusiasts – one of the oldest thrifty tips of all.

The need for thrift did not prevent poorer people from entering flower and produce shows with pride from the nineteenth century onwards. On this subject Dean Hole tells a tale of self-sacrifice in *About Roses* (1901): 'From a lady who lives near Nottingham ... I heard a far more striking instance of this floral devotion than the florists themselves. While conversing with the wife of a mechanic during the coldest period of a recent winter, she observed that the parental bed appeared to be scantily and insufficiently clothed, and she inquired if there were no more blankets in the house. "Yes, ma'am, we've another," replied the housewife; "but ..." and here she paused. "But what?", said the lady. "It is not at home, m'am." "Surely, surely it's not in pawn?" "Oh dear no, ma'am; Tom has only just took it – just took it –" "Well, Bessie, took it where?" "Please, ma'am, he took it – took it – took it to keep the frost out of the greenhouse; and please, ma'am, we don't want it, and we're quite hot in bed." ' Dean Hole fails to mention whether the plants in the greenhouse won any of the coveted prizes.

New Shoots

Seeds

SEED SAVING

Seed saving dates from the time when man started to cultivate rather than just hunt and gather. Excavations around Jericho suggest that the population were cultivating crops as early as 8000 BC.

To save seed, you need to leave seed heads and pods on the plants until mature. Philip Miller advises in *The Gardener's Dictionary* (1731): 'There are but few People so curious as they should be, in saving of their Seeds: some, for want of Judgment, do not distinguish the best Plants of their Kinds, to let grow for Seeds; and others out of Covetousness, to save a great Quantity of Seeds, frequently let a whole Spot of Ground, filled with any particular Sort of Plants, run to Seed; so that the good and bad Plants are saved indifferently, which is the Occasion of the general Complaint of the Badness of the Seeds which are commonly vended, and is what the Dealers in Seeds should endeavour to remedy.' Weed out poor specimens, save the finest for seed and mark them with coloured string or wool, as once your chosen plants have finished flowering or producing it will be nigh impossible to remember which plants they are.

Miller continues: 'All sorts of Seeds will keep much longer in their Pods, or outer Coverings, where they can be thus preserved; because the Covering not only preserves them from the Injuries of the outward Air, but if the Seeds are not Separated from them, they supply them with Nourishment, and thereby keep them plump and fair.' It is indeed a good idea to store them entire, although Miller is not correct in saying that they receive nourishment at this stage. 'But the Seeds of all soft Fruits, such as Cucumbers, Melons, etc., must be cleansed from the Fruit and Mucilage which surrounds them; otherwise the rotting of these Parts will corrupt and decay the Seeds in a short-time.' The best cleanser for small seeds is a bird's digestive system; however, rather than leaving the process to chance, you can wait until such seeds are fully if not overripe and then cleanse them in water and dry them thoroughly. Miller's concluding advice is: 'When Seeds are gathered, it should always be done in dry Weather; when there is no Moisture upon them; and then they should be hung up in Bags (especially

those which Vermin eat), in a dry Room.' The refrigerator is ideal for storing seeds, if you have room; or when they are fully dry you can store them in an old cake tin.

If you are looking to save a specific variety, follow Miller's advice for saving seeds of 'Roman or Christian Broccoli: In order to save good Seeds of this Kind of Broccoli in England, you should reserve a few of the largest Heads of the first Crop, which should be let remain to run up to Seed and all the Under-shoots should be constantly stripped off, leaving only the main Stem to flower and feed. If this be duly observed, and no other Sort of Cabbage permitted to feed near them, the Seeds will be as good as those procured from abroad, and the Sort may be preserved in Perfection for many Years.' The principle of selecting the best specimens for seed is excellent for any vegetable, flower or tree. For vegetal purity, grow different types of each vegetable in different areas.

In *The English Gardener* (1829) Cobbett advises on saving seed of various vegetables. On spinach, he says: 'Everyone knows the use of this excellent plant. Pigs, who are excellent judges of the relative qualities of vegetables, will leave cabbages for lettuces, and lettuces for spinage … As to saving the seed of the spinage, a few plants of each sort will be sufficient. The plants must be pulled up before the seed be dead ripe, or the birds will have every grain. It is a coarse-looking seed, with a thick husk upon it; but the small birds are very fond of it, and will begin to hammer it out of the husks while these are still green. The seed plants, when pulled up, should be laid in the sun to become perfectly dry, and the seed should be then rubbed off and put by in a dry place.'

Echoing Miller's advice, he continues: 'To save carrot seed, as well as beet-seed, you must take some of the last year's plants, and put them out early in the spring. When the seed is ripe, the best way is, with regard to the carrot, to cut off the whole stalk, hang it up in a very dry place, and there let it remain until you want the seed to sow. Kept in this way, it will grow very well at the end of three or four years; but, if separated from the stalk, it will not keep well for more than one year.'

ABOVE *From Hilderic Friend's* Flowers and Flower Lore *(1886), an engraving of a wallflower, the Victorian emblem of fidelity in misfortune because it fixes itself upon a dreary wall.*

For celery, Cobbett instructs: 'To have the seed of celery, take one plant or two, in the spring, out of the ridge that stands last. Plant it in an open place, and it will give you seed enough for several years; for the seed keeps good for ten years at least, if kept pretty much from the air, and in a dry place.'

EXCHANGE AND SALE

Though we do not know if they swapped seeds, several medieval writers promote the idea. Walter of Henley, in 1250, writes: 'Seed grown on other ground will bring more profit than that which is grown on your own. Will you see this? Plough two selions at the same time, and sow the one with seed which is bought and the other with corn which you have grown: in August you will see that I speak truly.'

Thomas Tusser in *Five Hundred Points of Good Husbandry* (1573) says:

> Good huswifes in sommer will save their owne seedes,
> against the next yeere, as occasion needes.
> One seede for another, to make an exchange,
> with fellowlie neighbourhood seemeth not strange.

John Gerard, Master of the Company of Barber Surgeons, who had a large garden in the Holborn district of London where he grew such novelties as double-flowering peaches and white-flowering thyme and, he claimed, over 1,000 plant varieties, enthusiastically engaged in seed and plant saving and swapping. Describing ruby chard in his *Herball or Generall Historie of Plantes* of 1597, he writes: 'Of Beets There is … another sort … red of colour … It grew with me 1596 to the height of eight cubits, and did bring forth his rough and uneven seed very plentifully: with which plant nature doth seeme to play and sport herselfe: for the seeds taken from that plant, which was altogether of one colour and sowen, doth bring forth plants of many and variable colours, as the worshipfull Gentleman master John Norden can very well testifie: unto whom I gave some of the seeds aforesaid, which in his garden brought forth many other of beautifull colours.'

Philip Miller exchanged plants and seeds from the Chelsea Physic Garden internationally and with English nurseries such as James Gordon of Mile End.

Today the Heritage Seed Library embodies the principle of seed exchange on a large scale: part of the HDRA The Organic Organisation, it saves old and unusual vegetable varieties for posterity, also distributing them to its members. And botanic gardens and other specialist gardeners with rare seeds share their stock in the hopes of bettering the chances of more plants being available. Every good gardener knows that by sharing your seeds and cuttings with friends you increase your chances of never losing favourite plants – as Thomas Jefferson did. He wrote to George Divers on 22 April 1826:

> You perhaps noticed in the newspapers some 3 or 4 months ago the mention of cucumbers in a particular garden in Ohio which measured 2½f. and 3.f. in length. Having a friend in that quarter I wrote and requested him to procure and send me some seed from one of the identical cucumbers. He has sent it, and to multiply chances of securing it, I send you 9 seeds, secured that nobody will be more likely to succeed than yourself. As soon as the days lengthen so that I can get back in the evening I shall come and ask in person how you all do.

The initial commercial seed exchanges were between great estates and monasteries. After the Dissolution of the Monasteries in 1539, the first nurseries took over the monasteries' role, offering seeds and plants for sale. The oldest surviving seedsman's catalogue is Londoner William Lucas's of *c.* 1677 and there were three major seedsman in London by 1688. Nursery numbers slowly increased; by 1800 they had become commonplace, Suttons & Sons, Reading, founded by John Sutton in 1806, being a typical example.

In 1903 William Unwin started to sell his first seeds – sweet peas – and eleven years later his son, Charles, joined him. In 1914 they produced their first catalogue of sweet peas, gladioli, dahlias, 167 varieties of vegetables and 27 varieties of salads and herbs. The average price was 2d. or 3d. a packet. Some seeds were sold in ounces and some in pints. Black-and-white pictures were used to enhance the 1920s catalogues and by 1932 colour had been introduced. Unwins sold seed by mail order to keen gardeners not only in Britain but also all round the world. Reputedly the only surviving family seedsmen, Unwins still offer the same choice, if not the same varieties.

John Parkinson observes in his 1629 *Paradisi in Sole Paradisus Terrestris*: 'Redish, Lettice, Carrots, Parsneps, Turneps, Cabbages, and Leekes ... our English seede ... is better than any that cometh from beyond the seas.' If you are buying seed, it is still a good idea to try to find seed varieties that include a local name, as they will have evolved characteristics to withstand the local vagaries of your climate.

VIABILITY

With saved seeds, or indeed when finding an old packet, how do you check viability? Cobbett gives two pieces of sound advice: 'I incline to the opinion that we should try seeds as our ancestors tried witches; not by fire, but by water; and that, following up their practice, we should reprobate and destroy all that do not readily sink … seeds of all sorts are … part sound and part unsound; … the proportion of each should be ascertained. Count … a hundred seeds, taken promiscuously and put them in water … If fifty sink and fifty swim, half your seed is bad, and half good.' Alternatively, he suggests that you ascertain 'the soundness or unsoundness of seed … by sowing them. If you have a hot-bed (or, if not, how easy to make one from a hand-glass), put a hundred seeds … sow them in a flower-pot, and plunge the pot in the earth, under the glass, in the hot-bed, or hand-glass. The climate, under the glass, is warm; and a very few days will tell you what proportion of your seed is sound.' A warm windowsill or greenhouse would suffice.

ABOVE *A grand label to inspire confidence in the customer that Webb's seeds were second to none.*

SOWING

The right timing of sowing is crucial for a good crop. If a plant is not hardy, for instance, it should not be sown until after the last frost, the timing of which varies from area to area. Those with a climate similar to that of East Anglia, effectively zone 9, would do well to follow Tusser's advice for gardeners in that area for peas:

> Who pescods would gather, to have with the last,
> to serve for his houshold till harvest be past,
> Must sowe them in Maie, in a corner ye shal,
> where through so late growing no hindrance may fal.

Today we tend simply to distinguish seeds requiring immediate sowing from the majority that are stored, with advice on germination and sowing requirements. Curiously Philip Miller divides his seeds into six categories: seeds to sow the autumn they were collected; seeds to sow the following spring; seeds to sow after one year, two years and three years (including melons and cucumbers); and seeds that may take over a year to germinate after sowing – especially umbellifers. He wrote ten pages on melon cultivation, which include an extraordinary piece of advice on what to do if you are unable to obtain three-year-old melon seed: '... if you are ... obliged to sow new ones; then you should either carry it in your Breeches Pocket, where it may be kept warm, ... by which means the watery parts will be carried off ... as hath been experienced by several curious Persons.'

As Thomas Hill succinctly instructs in *The Gardener's Labyrinth* (1577): 'The owner or Gardener ought to remember, that before he committeth seeds to the earth, the beds be disposed and troden out, into such a breadth and length, as best answereth to every plant root.' His observation is correct in that when it germinates a seed gently pushes out a radicle or root before risking its first seedling leaves. This radicle acts as an anchor, not making an extensive voyage of discovery but establishing an initial source of nutrient. For this reason when preparing a seed bed, after digging over, ensure that you firm the soil by treading and just rake the surface loose again.

A seed should be sown in its own depth of soil and would be very happy to be placed as Pliny advises in his *Naturalis Historia* of the first century AD: '... take the round treddles of a goat, and make in every one of them a little hole, putting therein the seed either of leeks, rocket, lettuce, parsley, endive

The dress code for sowing seeds remains almost unchanged. TOP: *Schoolgirls* c. *1920 rake the soil into a fine tilth, sow and label methodically.* BELOW: *Thomas Hill's Elizabethan gardeners demonstrate technical ability with a metal-edged spade and large wooden rake.*

or garden cresses, and close them up, and so put them it the ground.' Goats' droppings don't have the heat of horses'. If passing goats and horses are at a premium, remember that the point is that a seed likes to be enclosed, whether in firmed earth, a thumb pot or seed tray. A similar tip given in Victorian gardening books is to sow seeds into compost-filled eggshells. Gardeners later adapted this tip by using cardboard egg boxes, but now in these days of plastic egg boxes, what could be better than to recycle your empty eggshells into perfect seed-germinating pots? On the other side of the Atlantic, in spring the Huron Indians traditionally made baskets of bark, which they filled with rotten wood from old tree stumps in which they placed pumpkin seeds. These were then hung over a gentle fire until the seeds germinated, warm and fumigated.

An anonymous Victorian writer suggested in 1890: '... a safe plan is to sow about five seeds on reversed pieces of sod about 4 inches square. On planting in the ground, insert the sod with the growing plants, and firm the soil in the usual way.' This would be an excellent way of tucking in annuals where there were gaps after early flowering perennials or vegetables.

Leonard Meager addresses the need to handle seeds carefully, whether sowing directly into the ground or into pots, trays or eggshells. In *The English Gardner* (1670) he writes: 'if you put your seeds in a white Paper, you may (if the seeds are small) very easily and equally sow them by shaking the lower end of your paper with the forefinger of that hand you sow with; the paper must not be much open toward the end.'

GERMINATION

Describing seed germination, John Ray (1627–1705), dubbed by historian Dr Richard Pulteney 'the Aristotle of England and the Linnaeus of his age', writes:

> For as the seed of a plant when ripe falls to the ground and through lying loose does (as I saw) first receive its nourishment by the pores of its legumens and afterwards strikes root into the earth, so likewise the seed and egg of a viviparous animal, when ripened as it were by the male, drops off one of the ovaria into the womb where it lives for a while loose or free, without any adhesion to or connexion with the womb, drawing its nourishment through its involving membranes, then striking root into the womb.

On the same subject, Tusser uses an excellent analogy:

What is sown, as Seeds, are Plants compacted in a very little Space: and if they are too soon gorged with Moisture, that is faster than they can spend it upon their fibrous Root or Tendrils with which they lay hold on the Earth, they are apt to discompose their inwards Parts, and, in plain English, burst. But what is sett, namely Plants (for Beans, Pease, etc., ought not to be sett too wet, any more than other Seeds) have already Moisture in them, and their Texture is already expanded, and in its Shape: these require immediate strong Food, as being out of the Womb: and if their Nurse be dry, insted of getting from her, she sucks the little Moisture they have from them.

Sir Edward Salisbury furthers the analogy between seeds and humans when in *The Living Garden*, which he wrote in the 1930s, he describes the difference between a broad bean or lupin seeds, which have a well-formed embryo, and viburnum, mahonia or castor-oil seeds, which contain a small embryo but a greater food sac. He says: 'In all seeds, a certain amount of food is placed by the parent plant as a sort of trading capital on which the young plant, when it grows, can earn compound interest. But in some kinds of plants this food material is absorbed by the baby plant before the seeds pass into the dormant state, whilst in other kinds the food material is not so transferred until after the seed begins to germinate. The difference is comparable to that between a baby going to sleep with a bottle of milk by its bedside, which it will promptly consume on waking, and a baby that drinks its bottle of milk before it goes to sleep. The food is equally there in both instances during sleep, but in one case outside the baby and in the other case within.' Of course this description assumes that the baby is tucked up in a warm bed, not cold earth.

The Victorians made ivory tweezers with which the elegant gardener could prick out germinated seedlings.

Cuttings

CLONES

The Times, Saturday 4 May 1907, observes: 'There are some plants that can be so easily increased by other means that it is scarcely worth while to sow seed of them when once a few have been obtained; and there are also plants, as, for instance, most bulbs, which, if raised from seed, take years before they flower. But all means of propagation, even in the case of plants most easily increased, are strangely neglected by many gardeners.' A cutting will replicate its parent exactly, so when you find a favourite flower, it is worth perpetuating it and its virtues – such as an aromatic perfume or delicious taste – by taking cuttings.

Henry Bright, whose *A Year in a Lancashire Garden* was published in 1901, stayed in and took cuttings from some very smart establishments. 'I never stay anywhere, where there is a garden, without bringing back with me some one or more shrubs, as a remembrance of a beautiful place or happy hours; and, when I plant them, I fasten to them a label, mentioning their old home, and thus I am reminded – now of a quaint low house covered with creepers and nestling among the hills of Wales – now of a magnificent castle with its pleasance in the north of Ireland – now of a great hall in Scotland, where a wild glen runs down past the garden to the woods – now of an old English abbey, where the flowers of to-day spring up among the ruins of a thousand years ago.' This is a delightful idea, but remember that to take a living souvenir good guests must have the agreement of the garden's owner; discreetly pinching a cutting is theft.

METHODS

When taking cuttings, having checked that the parent plant is healthy and disease free, you need to choose a method. The simplest method, known as Irishman's cuttings, is to cut part of a plant where there is already some form of root, wild strawberries being a good example. Tusser was keen on these:

> Wife, into thy garden, and set me a plot,
> with strawberry rootes, of the best to be got:
> Such growing abroade, among thornes in the wood,
> wel chosen and picked proove excellent good.

The *Times* article quoted above makes the point that:

Nothing is easier ... than to get a large stock from a few plants of tufted pansies by simply taking off little rooted pieces and planting them in a cool place in light soil, keeping them well watered until they are established. If this is done as early as possible and when the ground is thoroughly wet with rain, the offsets will soon make good roots and be strong plants ready to plant out in the autumn. This method may be employed with most plants that increase by means of rooted tufts or offsets, and it is often better than division, since it leaves the parent plant undisturbed.

Layering follows the Irishman's theme in that the 'cutting' stays attached to the parent, pegged to the ground, until it has rooted. This is an ideal method for slow-rooting herbs such as sweet bay and wall germander – the latter being, as Friar Henry Daniel noted in the 1360s, 'nowhere but of setting or sowing, and of sowing but elvish'.

Splitting or dividing herbaceous plants not only provides more plants but invigorates your stock. Daniel recommends this for the squill onion in the *Scilla* family, which was used as a vegetable and a medicine until the late seventeenth century: 'Squylle It is wonder like Leek, save greater and higher and flowered wonder like, but it seedeth not but dwineth away. It multiplieth only ... in root as doeth Saffron.' Saffron was once used to line vegetable beds in the belief that passing feet squashed the bulbs, which encouraged new bulblets to form in the damaged areas, in effect dividing them.

The tip of a plant is full of new life and the plant's most disease-free part. Given shelter from drying winds and

An Edwardian illustration of 'layering by circumposition' and another use for a broken pot.

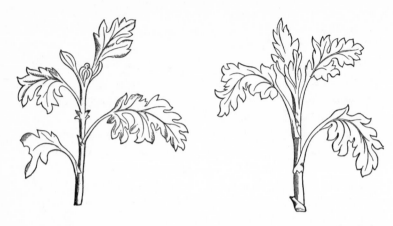

Tip cuttings, from plants such as this chrysanthemum, root better if cut directly under a bud, as seen in the right-hand drawing.

direct sun a tip cutting will root quickly. In 1888 Edwin Molyneux guided the enthusiastic Victorian chrysanthemum grower on how to take and successfully root cuttings, and ensure healthy growth afterwards: 'They should be about 3 inches long, not too sappy, and cut square across below a joint. Stout suckers find favour with some growers – namely, growths that push through the soil and taken off when about 2 inches long with bristling roots attached.' You could try taking a cutting of any plant from a bouquet for a wedding or other memorable occasion. Just treat a stem as a tip cutting and hope for the best. Remember to pinch out all emerging flowers and flower buds first.

Heel cuttings are slower to take root but end-of-the-year favourites. You take a cutting from new growth with just a heel of mature wood. In the rose section of his *Handy Book of The Flower-Garden* (1868), David Thomson, gardener to Lady Mary C. Nisbet Hamilton, recommends raising roses from heel cuttings rather than budding them on to root stocks: 'The propagation … by cuttings, is nearly as easy as the propagation of Gooseberry or Currant in the open border, without any protection whatever. From the middle of September to the middle of October is the best time … In taking the cuttings, those that have well matured their growth, and are strong and straight, should be selected. And in detaching these from the parent plants, take with them a small portion of the previous year's growth; and in doing this it is readily understood how not many cuttings should be removed near to one another, or the parent plant will be mutilated.' For this reason it is worth combining pruning with taking cuttings.

Thomson continues: 'In making the cuttings, cut their base cleanly through, just where the season's growth has started from, taking rather a thin slice of last year's wood to form a heel to the cutting; they should then be shortened to 9 or 10 inches in length [the top should have a slanting cut away from the top bud] and are in this condition ready for being put into the ground. And the best way to put them in is … in rows a foot apart, and from 5 to 6 inches between each cutting, and so deep as only to have three or four eyes above ground, – fixing each row well in the ground … those who can afford to give them the protection of a frame or handglasses had better do so …[You will have] beautifully rooted plants by midsummer … in November … run out into nursery lines a foot or so apart each way … or they may be planted in the beds at once … Those who can command pots and pans with a gentle bottom heat, can root them at midsummer, as soon as the plants have shed their first crop of bloom …' If you plan to take lots of autumn cuttings it is worth preparing a cuttings trench, incorporating lots of fibrous material (coir or peat substitutes) and sharp sand or vermiculite for drainage.

Root cuttings from roots and runners should include the dormant buds, which will in turn root and send up leaves. It is these buds that enable the gardener's deadly enemies ground elder and bindweed to return with a vengeance if one or two are left in the ground after weeding. In autumn and winter try lifting large-rooted plants after their leaves have died back and breaking or cutting a piece of root into wedges each with at least one bud. To break or cut, that is the question: some roots break cleanly, while it is easier to cut others. Use a sharp knife or secateurs, as ragged or rough cuts are more susceptible to rot and disease. You can experiment with many large-rooted plants.

In his *Herball* of 1597 Gerard recommends this method for the plant that sprang from Helen of Troy's tears when Paris left her: 'The herb Elecampane may not be sown, in that the seeds bestowed in beds prosper not, but rather set the young buds broken tenderly from the root, in earth wel dunged and laboured afore. And those begin to set in the month of February, well three foot asunder one from the other, in that those send forth big leaves, and long roots spreading in the earth.' Elecampane (*Inula helenium*) originated in meadows, so it thrives in deep, moisture-retentive soil, and is an architectural addition to a border.

HEALTHY CUTTINGS

Good stock is essential for propagation but sometimes we have to work with sad remnants. The obstetrician, anatomist and physician James Douglas (1675–1748) evocatively describes Hoxton nurseryman Thomas Fairchild's efforts to propagate the newly introduced *Lilio narcissus* (probably an amaryllis): 'When the roots arrived in London they were very much wasted and decayed, but falling by good luck into the hands of the most ingenious and skilful Mr. Fairchild of Hoxton, he with surpassing care and pains recovered them. A surgeon could not have treated a mortified animal member with more judgment and dexterity than he showed in his management of this corrupted vegetable. He cautiously separated the mortified parts from the sound and, by the application of artificial heat, cherished and recovered the small remains of life, and thus by degrees brought them to that healthful and thriving state in which we now behold them.' It is better to take a small, well-honed clean cutting than one with any detritus or unsound growth.

If you have access to a propagation box or heated cuttings bed, as Fairchild did, cuttings root most efficiently with hot bottoms, misty middles and cool tops. In *The Ladies Companion to the Flower Garden* (1846) Jane Loudon illustrates two methods of giving cuttings vapour:

> Mr. Alexander Forsyth, gardener to the Earl of Shrewsbury, at Alton Towers, recommends the following plan: Take a wide-mouthed forty-eight sized pot, and put some potsherds at the bottom in the usual manner. Then take a wide-mouth small sixty, and put a piece of clay in the bottom, to stop the hole, and then place it inside the other, so that the tops of both pots may be on a level. The space between the pots must then be filled in with sand or other soil, and the cuttings inserted ... The inner pot should be filled with water, and the outer pot may then be plunged in the ground, or into a hotbed, and covered with a glass or not, according to the nature of the cutting.

Sharp sand drains well and helps a cutting to callous, but fibrous compost would be better, as new roots will become long and fine in sand, whereas a fibrous compost encourages lots of small roots, and more root hairs to draw nutrients out of the soil and fibrous roots and feed the new plant. The second method, 'Fyffe's Mode' (illustrated opposite), would be my recommendation, again with a fibrous compost as a substitute for peat or moss.

Mrs Loudon's recommended modes of rooting: LEFT *Forsyth's (see page 46) and* RIGHT *Fyffe's. This, she says, '… is to have a small pot (a sixty), b, turned upside down in a larger pot (a thirty-two), a, and to have the space c filled with small pebbles; e is a layer of peat, earth or moss, and d a covering of sand. This kind of pot is very useful for all cuttings that are liable to damp off, as the water trickles down through the pebbles; and if the pot be placed in bottom heat, the hot vapour rises through the pebbles in the same way, without burning the roots.'*

Budding and grafting

If BBC Radio Four invited you on to the famed desert island and, apart from listening to your ten favourite pieces of music, you found yourself reading the Bible and Shakespeare, you would find that both offer insights on the nature of grafting.

In the Book of Romans, St Paul explains: 'For if the first fruits be holy, the lump is also holy: and if the root be holy, so are the branches. And if some of the branches be broken off, and thou, being a wild olive tree, wert graffed in among them [you would partake] of the root and fatness of the olive tree.'

In Shakespeare's *The Winter's Tale*, Polixenes describes how

> … we marry
> A gentler scion to the wildest stock
> And make conceive a bark of baser kind
> By bud of noble race: this is an art
> Which does mend nature, – change it rather; but
> The art itself is nature.

Whereas the craft of grafting fuses a branch or twig on to a host tree or shrub, the later skill of budding is a form of grafting that just uses a bud, which is slipped into a pocket incised in the bark.

libII. *VIRGIL'S GEORGICKS.*

This late seventeenth- or early eighteenth-century engraving for Virgil's Georgics shows that the Greeks knew all about taking buds and grafting. The digging looks unnecessarily primitive and painful.

Eleven grafting implements. In the second half of the nineteenth century Great Exhibitions took place around the world, demonstrating tools for every conceivable task.

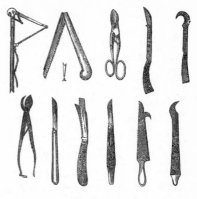

Fitzherbert's *Book of Husbandry* (1534) extols the virtues of skilled domestic grafting: 'It is necessarye, profytable, and also a pleasure, to a housbande, to have peares, wardens, and apples of dyuerse sortes. And also cheryes, filberdes, bulleys, dampsons, plummes, walnuttes, and such another. And therefore it is convenyent to lerne howe thou shalte graffe.'

The ever-observant Pliny describes good times for grafting being when the earth is 'in love':

> Like as therefore there be three seasons of planting trees, so there are as many wherein they bud and put forth new shoots; to wit, the spring, the rising of the Dog star, and the apparition of Arcturus. And verily this is a thing worthy to be noted, that not only beasts and other living creatures have an appetite to engender, but the earth also, and the plants thereupon, are much more lusty and hot that way. And therefore to make them to conceive in due season, the time would be well observed, when they be as it were in love and desire the act of generation. And not only in the earth and trees therein planted, is this to be seen, but in grafts and stocks also particularly by themselves, since that they have a mutual and respective appetite, one to join and incorporate with the other.

In *A Short and Sure Guide in the Practice of Raising and Ordering of Fruit Trees* (short and sure being an approach many Victorian writers would have done well to follow), published in 1672, F. Drope writes about how to bud oranges with an inverted T incision, and like Pliny he understood the importance of grafting in spring with scions: 'The sap, arriving at the outside of the wood, there to generate a new orbe, doth in the restagnation seize upon and conjoine itself to the moist part of the graft, that is affinity unto it.'

Cobbett's textural illustration of T budding,
where an incision in the shape of a T is made in
the host branch to accommodate a favoured bud,
best done in July/August.

TO GRAFT OR NOT TO GRAFT

The 'climbing' red and white roses that are a feature of medieval portraits of the Virgin Mary were in fact Gallica roses budded on to briar or eglantine stocks. Their life was short but the effect was good. However William Robinson in his 'Preface to the New Edition' of *The English Flower Garden* (1883) – which remains one of the best gardening books, especially if you enjoy someone not afraid to voice their prejudices – sounds the call to arms against the 'Evils of' grafting roses:

> Disastrous for all lands, to me the art of grafting is most so in England, as ours is the country of the rose in continuous bloom.
>
> In New England, or in Italy, Canada and other countries, where the Rose bloom is burnt up in the summer heat, in our cool land she goes on in her beauty all the summer. In my garden we have Roses in all their beauty from June until well into October. One gets this only when the Rose is growing on its natural root.
>
> This prolonged bloom is the greatest gain. One evil of grafting is a short life. On their natural root they will live as long as men do now, but on the grafted stock the life is a short one. Some Roses never show their beauty in a grafted state. I never knew what a fine Rose Madame Hoste was until I saw it growing in the station-yard where there was no clay near. Pharisaer, a beautiful Rose, was deformed on the briar and had to be thrown away in a few years. On its natural root is it a lovely and stately Rose for many years.

'Pharisaer' is a fragrant pastel Hybrid Tea that was introduced in 1903 and is still flourishing. Today some rosarians claim that a rose's life is lengthened by grafting but increasingly the method is not used.

Since earliest times gardeners have believed that top fruits can be improved by grafting. The gardens of Bishop Guillaume de Passavant at Le Mans 1145–58 were planted, according to a contemporary, 'with many sorts of trees for grafting foreign fruits, equally lovely; for those leaning out of the hall windows to admire the beauty of the trees, and others in the garden'.

In *A History of Gardening in England* (1895) Alicia Amherst describes how gardeners at the time of John Gardener, who wrote *The Feate of Gardening, c.* 1440, paid great attention to grafting fruit:

The art of grafting a pear on a hawthorn was known at a very early period. John Gardener directs the stocks for grafts of both apples and pears to be planted in January, the apple on an apple stock, and the pear 'apon a haw-thorne'. The grafting, he says, should take place any time between September and April.

> Wyth a saw thou schalt the tre kytte
> And with a knyfe smowth make hytte
> Klene a-tweyne the stok of the tre
> Where-yn that thy graffe schall be
> Make thy Kyttyng' of thy graffe
> By-twyne the newe & the olde staffe.

Seventeenth-century Ralph Austen was well aware of the advantages of marrying tough stock to desirable scions. In *A Treatise of Fruit Trees*, he says:

That although it be true that the Northern Counties lie in a more cold Climate than Worcestershire, Herefordshire, and those Fruit Countries, yet I doubt not but that if they were as diligent in planting Fruit-trees in the North parts ... they might have a store of good fruit ... both Apples, Pears, Cherries which yearly experience shewes endure cold, and come to perfection in cold springs when many other kinds are spoyled ... Procure Grafts, or Young trees ready grafted of best bearing kinds, such as are found by experience to beare well, even in cold spring ... Let such sorts be sought for and planted.

In John Gardener's time, Alicia Amherst tells us, 'Clay had to be laid on the stock, "to kepe the rayne owte", and moss bound over the clay with "a wyth of haseltree rynde".' By 1833 methods had become more sophisticated. In *The English Gardener* William Cobbett gives a recipe for 'Grafting Wax Take of pitch and resin four parts each; beeswax two parts; tallow one part; melt and mix these ingredients, and use them for grafting when just warm.' Today we can buy a roll of plastic grafting tape.

Sustenance

Tree fruits

> What wond'rous Life is this I lead!
> Ripe Apples drop about my head;
> The Luscious Clusters of the Vine
> Upon my Mouth do crush their Wine;
> The Nectaren and curious Peach
> Into my hands themselves do reach;
> Stumbling on Melons, as I pass,
> Insnar'd with Flow'rs, I fall on Grass.
>
> Andrew Marvell, from 'Thoughts in a Garden'

What a shame that Adam and Eve lived several thousand years too early to be inspired by *A Treatise of FRUIT-TREES Shewing the manner of Grafting, Setting, Pruning, and Ordering of them in all respects: According to divers new and easy*

A postcard of c. 1910, *purportedly of Thomas à Becket's 750-year-old fig. Figs are rarely grown as orchard trees, fruiting better with their roots constricted.*

Rules of experience; gathered in ye space of twenty yeares. Whereby the value of Lands may be much improved, in a shorttime, by small cost, and little labour. Also discovering some dangerous Errors, both in ye Theory and Practise of ye Art of Planting Fruit:trees with the Alimentall and Physicall use of fruits. Together with The Spirituall Use of an Orchard: Held forth in divers Similitudes betweene Naturall & spirituall Fruit:trees: according to Scripture & Experience by R.A. Austen Practiser in Ye Art of Planting.

Ralph Austen's prose of 1653 describing the pleasures of growing fruit trees reads almost like poetry, a balm for post-Civil War England:

> Vineyards, orchards, gardens and such enclosed plots are the flowers, starres and paradises of the earth … The World is a great Library, and Fruit-trees are some of the Bookes wherein we may read & see plainly the Attributes of God his Power, Wisdome, Goodnesse, Etc. and be instructed and taught our duty towards him in many things even from Fruit-trees for (in a Metaphoricall sence) they are Bookes, so likewise in the same sence they have a Voyce, and speake plainely to us, and teach many good lessons … The Ancients were skilled in this kind of Learning, in teaching by SIMILITUDES, and one of them observes, that God sent us the Booke of Nature, before he sent us the Book of the Scriptures.

Later in his 'Eight divine arguments of the dignity and value of Fruit-trees' he observes: 'Oh how sweet and pleasant is the fruit of those Trees which a man hath planted and ordered with his owne hand, to gather it, and largely and freely bestow and distribute it among his kindred and friends.'

Three hundred years later Marion Cran shares his sentiment when in *Garden Wisdom* she writes: 'No fruit tastes so sweet as that we pull from the tree we planted ourselves! An apple has a rarer taste if we remember and have shared in the care that has gone to its rounding and ruddying. There are those who call this feeling 'sentiment', and even 'bosh'; but it remains a fact.'

Likewise the Durham clergyman William Lawson enjoyed growing fruit. The mounts lining his garden were constructed from boughs of trees and soil planted up with plums, Kentish cherry and damsons; in *A New Orchard and Garden* (1618) he also describes borders 'hanging and drooping' with raspberries, barberries and currants as well as roses and other berries. He laid out his orchard with geometrical precision in a series of fives or quincunx forms (see overleaf) for quince, apple and pear trees and describes it as an 'unspeakable pleasure, and infinite commoditie'.

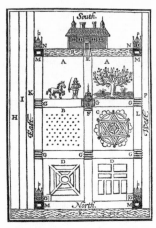

GROWING FRUIT TREES

Many writers give advice on how to create an orchard. In his *Gardener's Dictionary* Philip Miller says: 'The soil I would in general advise to be used for all Sort of Fruit-trees, is fresh untried Earth from a Pasture-ground, taken about ten Inches deep, with the Turf, and laid to rot and mellow at least twelve Months, before it is used; and this must be kept often turned, to sweeten and imbibe the nitrous Particles of the Air.' Turf has lots of nutrients and helps to make the soil moisture-retentive.

In *The English Garden* Cobbett suggests planting a catch crop around a tree as it matures, instructing: 'As to the cultivation of orchards, ... first put manure to a good distance round the tree ... plough up the whole of the land, to manure it, and to take a crop or two of grain ... after this ... lay the land down with grass again.' Ralph Austen also recommends grass for orchards: 'Mowing of grounds yearly, where Fruit-trees grow, is exceedingly prejudicial to Trees (unless the soil be very fertile). But pasturing of Orchards and Grounds where Fruit-trees grow, is observed to be of great advantage to their prosperity, and bearing fruits.'

Note, however, Robert Thompson's advice in *The Gardener's Assistant*, first published in the 1880s: 'Grass growing over, or in close proximity to, the roots of newly-planted young fruit-trees is injurious to them, stunting the growth, starving the tree, and either crippling it for many years, or rendering it entirely useless.' Absolutely right. Initially the grass will compete with the fruit trees for moisture and nutrients; but once the trees are established, say after five years, the grass around them will be useful for slowing down the tree's growth.

When should you plant an orchard? Follow John Aubrey's seventeenth-century 'proverb for Apples, Peares, Hawthorns, Quicksetts, Oakes: Sett them at All-hallow-tide, and command them to grow, Sett them at Candlemas, and entreat them to grow'. In other words, preferably plant in November rather than February.

ABOVE *William Lawson's ideal garden plan. Note the pruned and trained standard apple in the top right-hand corner.*

Lawson advises leaving a great distance between each tree, as does Philip Miller:

> The Distance these Trees ought to be planted, is at least forty Feet square; that the Sun and Air may freely pass to the every Part of the Tree, to dissipate all crude and unhealthy Vapours, which are either exhaled from the Earth, or produced from the Perspiration of the Trees, and are many times the Cause of Blights ... and must occasion the Fruit to be crude and ill-tasted ... with their close standing we find vast Numbers of Orchards that have scarcely a healthy Tree in them, the greatest Part of them being either cankered, or covered over with Moss; and how can we suppose to eat kindly Fruit from distempered Trees? We may with as much Justice affirm, that a distempered Woman will give healthy Milk.

A.J. Downing, too, gives large planting distances in his *Cottage Residences* of 1842: 'Apples are found to thrive best in a strong loam, if stony it is preferable; pears and cherries, in a mellow, gravelly loam: plums in a strong clayey loam and peaches in a light sandy loam. Apples may be planted in an orchard at from 30 to 45 feet apart; cherries and pears, from 25 to 30 feet; peaches and plums, from 20 to 25 feet. In transplanting all fruit trees be mindful not to commit the common error of setting them too deep.'

Today top fruit is budded much higher, but it is always worth heeding the soil mark and planting to the same depth. Also, trees are now mostly budded on to dwarf stocks, which enables us to plant more closely, to as little as 3 feet (90 cm).

However, as Miller implies, the more air circulating around the branches the better for disease prevention, blossom setting and fruit ripening, so prune. Pruning will also help fruiting – indeed failure to prune is an 'Error', according to Miller: 'And since I am upon this Article of close Planting, suffer me to make a little Digression, not altogether foreign to our present Purpose; which is to take notice of a prevailing Error, in planting Fruit-gardens like Wilderness-trees, or Flowering-shrubs, close together, and mixing the different Sorts of Fruits in each Division, ... and suffering them to grow, as they are naturally disposed, without ever pruning them, hereby hoping to have great Quantities of Fruit with very little Trouble after the first Planting.' Encouraging lateral growth of all top fruit tree branches slows down vertical growth and apical dominance, controlling the auxins and ensuring good fruiting. If you seek quality not quantity, prune back the fruiting wood after fruiting and leaf drop; also thin the crop in early summer. Miller advises 'that it is impossible for a Person, let him be ever so well skilled in Fruit trees, to reduce them into any tolerable Order by Winter-pruning only, if they are wholly neglected in the Spring'. Lawson illustrates 'The perfecte forme of an Apple tree ... for health, strength and productivity', with an open centre ensuring maximum penetration of sunshine and good air circulation (as illustrated on his garden plan on page 54).

Anyone growing fruit trees would do well to consult Thomas Rivers III. Born in 1798 into an established family of nurserymen at Sawbridgeworth, Hertfordshire, Rivers was as precocious as many of the fruit varieties he bred. Aged thirteen he noted that the fruit trees that were too weak or small for sale as standards fruited far better when transplanted by his grandfather and father. He spent his adolescence experimenting with root pruning and travelled around Europe. He also studied double grafting and rootstocks. Aged twenty-two he introduced the apples 'Rivers Broadleaved Paradise' and 'Nonsuch Paradise', dwarfing rootstocks that were ideal for pyramids and bushes; later East Malling Research Station renamed them Malling I and Malling VI. He imported many varieties from abroad for research and experimentation, including the apple 'Mother' (also known as 'American Mother') from the United States. He was one of the most prolific fruit breeders. His most famous introductions were the 'Conference' pear, 'Peregrine' peach and 'Czar', 'Early Rivers' and 'Monarch' plums.

Rivers recommended planting fruit trees at 10-foot (3-metre) centres, lifting them after ten years and transplanting. He also recommended transplanting, as well as root pruning, if trees were not producing fruit – a solution later endorsed in Thompson's *Gardener's Assistant*: 'The routine work comprises many matters in which the most watchful care must be exercised and if the trees fail to bear from excessive vigour, root pruning or lifting are laborious but usually effective remedies.' I moved a 'Conference' pear after twenty years into a sunnier spot and have been rewarded with quantity and quality.

APPLES AND PEARS

Henry VIII did much to promote the improvement of apple varieties. These had changed little in the 1,500 years since Pliny described twenty-two.

The saying 'He who plants pears, plants for his heirs' relates to large standard trees, which take more than twenty years to reach fruiting.

There is a French saying '*Manger poire, ne pas boire*' – in other words, pears are a good thirst quencher. Pears are also, after grapes, the most digestible fruit for an invalid to eat. (The plant hunter Robert Fortune, who introduced the Chinese gooseberry to New Zealand – where it enjoyed a twentieth-century makeover into the ubiquitous vitamin C-laden kiwi fruit – describes in his account of his travels how when visiting a Cantonese garden in 1842 he paused at the Library of Verdant Purity, where he noticed a fruit tree that bore a label saying 'Ramblers here will be excused plucking the fruit of this tree.')

The number of varieties continued to increase. By 1842 in *Cottage Residences* A.J. Downing writes:

Horticulture, but more especially pomology, that branch of it devoted to fruits, has received so much attention both in Europe and at home, that within the last 20 years the number of delicious fruits capable of being raised in the open air has been more than doubled. The Pear especially has been greatly improved and ameliorated, and has indeed taken the first rank among dessert fruits, in consideration of the variety in flavour, time of ripening, duration and beauty of the numerous sorts. The late autumn and winter varieties are a very valuable acquisition to our dessert at these seasons.

Rivers successfully bred the delicious and ubiquitous 'Conference' pear just before his death in 1877. It was named at the 1888 International Fruit Conference by his son, Thomas F. Rivers, and became readily available from 1894.

Fewer than thirty years later Thompson's *Gardener's Assistant* reckoned that there were 1,000 pear varieties available, sixty of which Thompson listed as 'Useful Pears'. When planting pears, remember his advice to think ornamental as well as practical:

As one of the most delicious dessert fruits at the command of the British cultivator, the Pear has attained a high degree of popularity amongst those fruits which are generally hardy in this climate.

A well-grown Pear-tree in full blossom is an exceedingly beautiful object … Another mode of utilizing Pears for ornamental purposes is that of training them over light metal or wooden arches. The various forms of upright cordons are well adapted for this purpose … It is desirable … to avoid narrow arches, which have a very meagre appearance and only prove disappointing.

Aspect is important in reference to Pear culture, the best dessert varieties, especially the early and midseason sorts, requiring the fullest exposure to sunlight to perfect them. The Pear demands a higher temperature than the Apple to develop its finest qualities … this is still further aided by a moderate slope towards the south.

That is why the French may not beat the English with apples but it is hard to match their pears.

Under 'Orchards', Thompson reports: 'Mr. T. Rivers has stated that 'Pear-trees on the Quince stock offer a curious anomaly, for if they are removed [translated] quite late in the spring – say towards the end of March, when their blossom-buds are just on the point of bursting – they will bear a fine and often an abundant crop of fruit the same season. This is perhaps owing to the blossoms being retarded, and thus escaping the spring frosts; but it has so often occurred when no frosts have visited us that I notice it, in fact no trees bear late removal so well as pears on Quince stocks.' If you did this, you would have to water and nurture extremely diligently to ensure that the blossoms did not drop from shock.

PLUMS

Gerard appears to have had sixty varieties of plums in his Holborn garden – in his 1597 *Herball* he writes: 'To write of Plums particularly would require a peculiar volume … Every clymate hath his owne fruite, far different from that of other countries; my selfe have threescore sorts in my garden, and all strange and rare' – although it is possible that he was including those in the substantial gardens he managed for the Cecils at Theobalds.

By comparison Philip Miller's list of thirty-two varieties including bullaces and sloes seems modest. He especially likes one of them: 'The Green Gage Plum. This is one of the best Plums in England; it is of a middle Size, round, and of a yellowish-green Colour on the Outside; the Flesh is firm, of a deep-green Colour, and parts from the Stone; the Juice has an exceeding rich Flavour; and it is a great Bearer: ripe the End of July.

This called Gros Damas verd, i.e. The great green Damask in France.'

Thomas Rivers imported 'Transparent Gage' and 'Oullins Golden Gage' from France and 'Dennistons Superb Gage' and 'Jefferson Gage' from the United States. Thompson describes the latter: 'Jefferson – Dessert. Late September. Fruit large, roundish-oval, dark-yellow, speckled with purple and red, bloom thin; flesh deep orange, juicy, exceedingly rich and sugary. Tree a good grower and excellent bearer, either in the open as a standard or bush in warm localities, or against a wall in colder parts. Of American origin.'

Rivers successfully raised the 'Early Rivers Prolific' plum, now known as 'Early Rivers', in 1834. He found it amongst a batch of seedlings from the tender 'Precoce de Tours'. He realized that by raising it from seed he had produced a hardy strain. It took eight to twelve years to fruit, but after 1845 when glass became cheaper (the tax on it was repealed in 1845) he was able to grow it under glass and speed up the process.

On the care of plums, Thompson advises: 'Plums, when planted in rich soil are likely to grow over-luxuriantly, and to bear little or no fruit. To remedy this, they should be lifted and replanted about the end of October. This checks the rank growth and induces the formation of fruit-buds. Trees when once brought into bearing condition rarely give further trouble; but, should they still be unfruitful, lift them again the following autumn and mix some lime rubble with the soil when replanting.' Note the timing of October, when you will avoid any risk of silver leaf disease as well as the reduction of leaf vigour in favour of fruit production. It is also true that once plums have fruited heavily, the cropping increases thereafter – spring frost permitting.

Thompson continues: 'The roots of Plum run near the surface, and on this account the ground must either be dug every year or not at all.' So once a plum is established, either let grass grow around it, in which you could grow bulbs, or prepare a bed and grow annual displays of flowers or vegetables.

WALL FRUIT

Although traditionally the fruit that tempted Eve was believed to be an apple, recent evidence suggests it was the more luscious apricot. This tender fruit became popular in England in the reign of Henry VIII, whose pleasure in the fruit's flesh encouraged noblemen to cultivate it in walled gardens. By

1748 Philip Miller was advising: 'We have in the English Gardens about eight Sorts of this Fruit cultivated; These Trees are ... planted against Walls, and should have an East or West Aspect; for if they are planted full South, the great Heat causes them to be mealy, before they are well eatable.'

In the early nineteenth century landowners had flues built into their kitchen garden walls to protect apricot blossom from frost, while in Oxfordshire and Northamptonshire they encouraged employees to plant apricot trees against their cottage chimney breasts. Jane Loudon notes: 'It often, indeed, happens that in districts where the apricot generally fails on the open wall it may often be seen flourishing against the gable end of a warmly-situated cottage or farmhouse.' Both measures are worth adopting as long as the aspect is right.

Although self-fertile, apricots may need help with pollination. In 1850 Thomas Rivers published *The Miniature Fruit Garden*, which details how to grow a wide range of fruits, and had gone into twenty editions by 1891. In it he suggests: 'Fertilisation of flowers may be aided by stroking over the flowers with a light feather brush such as housemaids use for dusting ornaments.'

TOP *Encyclopaedias such as Thompson's* Gardener's Assistant *encouraged readers to maximize every available surface.* BOTTOM *This winter shot of* c. 1915 *displays the skills of its owners, who could anticipate summers of gathering fresh fruit from every bedroom window.*

Henry A. Bright did well with apricots. In *A Year in a Lancashire Garden* (1901), he writes in August: 'The Apricots have done fairly, and were so early that we gathered three or four in the last days of July – a full month before their usual time. The Moorpark Apricot, which we owe to Sir William Temple, is still the best.'

He was not, however, successful with other wall fruit: 'It is, I find, a dangerous thing to leave a garden masterless for even a month ... My readers will hardly be interested by the details of my grievances; it is pleasanter to tell when we have been successful ... The wall fruit, however, I must mention. The ants and the aphids, and possibly some frost, have destroyed the Peach crop utterly. There is not a single Peach, and the Nectarines, which are certainly a hardier fruit with us, only number thirty in all.'

You might be interested in the peach if you want to grow fruit for its symbolism, for the Chinese venerate the peach as the promise of fecundity and immortality.

Whether or not you know the variety of a peach or nectarine you have eaten and particularly enjoyed you could try raising your own fruit from the stone. It is much easier than you might imagine. Be enthused by Rivers' advice: 'Royal George ... reproduces itself from seed with rare exceptions; ... Noblesse ... very rare to find the least deviation ...; Grosse Mignonne ... out of twenty seedlings it is rare to find much deviation from the parent

Potting peaches in 1903. Had they read Thomas Rivers' The Miniature Fruit Garden*? And do the tam o'shanters indicate apprenticeship or a mother's caution?*

stock; Walburton Admirable … reproduces itself from seed. There are numerous recorded instances of a Nectarine originating from the seed of a Peach, and vice versa.' Of these, 'Alexandra Noblesse' and 'Royal George' are still commercially available.

PROTECTING FRUIT

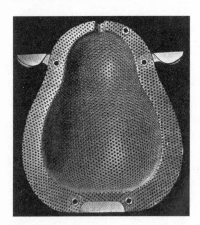 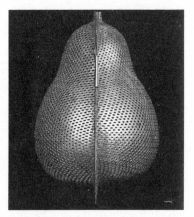

All fruit growers face the problem of birds and other animals and insects eating the fruit. Thompson has a sophisticated answer: 'The Cloister Fruit Protector is a device for protecting ripening fruit from injuries by birds, wasps, snails, etc. It is made of perforated celluloid, which is very light and neat in appearance, and is adapted for Pears, Apples, and other fruits. It is made in two parts with a flanged joint so that it can readily be applied without undue handling or bruising the fruit … closed by clamps fixed to the edges. It's as light as muslin, much more durable, having been continuously exposed in all kinds of weather, fierce sun and heavy winter rains, without the least injury.'

In the radio programme from which this book originated Bob Sherman described the special pouches his wife makes out of net curtains to protect his pears. A neighbour in France ties up all his pears and peaches in polythene bags, with small holes to stop overheating and rotting, and I tie unwanted computer discs to fruit trees to deter birds. Back in 1572 Mascall suggested putting a layer of ashes and unslaked lime around fruit trees then

ABOVE *The 'Cloister Fruit Protector' described in Thompson's* Gardener's Assistant: *'a device for protecting ripening fruit from injuries by birds, wasps, snails, etc.', made from perforated celluloid.*

shaking vigorously so that any pest falls into the mixture, where it can easily be identified and destroyed.

You might want to adapt a post-war Suffolk tip: people used to leave the grass uncut under their fruit trees until it was waist high, then set fire to it, thus smoking out insect predators. Take care, though, not to scorch the following season's fruit buds as well.

THE FRUITS OF YOUR LABOURS

During a European tour Thomas Jefferson visited Fontainebleau, near Paris, in 1785. In his journal he writes: 'After descending the hill again I saw a man cutting fern. I went to him under the pretence of asking the shortest road to

This tableau, taken by stereoscope (when two images are viewed together through binoculars to give a 3D effect), captures the role of the fruitful garden promoted by the Arts and Crafts movement.

the town, and afterwards asked for what use he was cutting fern. He told me that this part of the country furnished a great deal of fruit to Paris. That when packed in straw it acquired an ill taste, but that dry fern preserved it perfectly without communicating any taste at all. I treasured this observation for the preservation of my apples on my return to my own country.'

William Robinson, when revising Jane Loudon's *The Amateur Gardener* in

Successfully producing fruit is just the start: efficient harvest and storage requires skill and specialist equipment. Note the reference in the bottom line to the fruit protector described on page 62.

1880, added to it: 'In the month of February 1869, a few prizes brought together a considerable number of fine apples and pears from various exhibitors, and the fruit was in such good preservation that the mode of keeping it in the various cases was inquired into. The following is a précis, published by the Royal Horticultural Society.' Of the nine not exactly precise points that follow for gardeners with fruit stores, point eight is worthy of modern note: 'Where especially clear and beautiful specimens are wanted, they may be packed carefully in dry bran, or in layers of perfectly dry cotton-wool, either in closed boxes or in large garden pots. Scentless sawdust will answer the same purpose, but pine sawdust is apt to communicate an unpleasant taste.' This would be a good way to use large terracotta pots after summer bedding. Preferably you should store fruit in cool temperatures that do not fluctuate too greatly.

POTTED FRUIT

In 1852 Thomas Rivers published *The Orchard House or the Cultivation of Fruit Trees in Pots under Glass* (initially in aid of Sawbridgeworth church), which went into fifteen editions. The concept of the 'orchard house' was picked up by Beeton's *Shilling Gardening Book*: – 'Mr. Rivers, who is our best authority upon Orchard-houses, describes as a convenient form of house, a lean-to structure, 30 feet long and 12 feet 6 inches' – and Thompson's *Gardener's Assistant*:

> The Orchard House is the latest development of fruit-growing under glass, and it is chiefly owing to the efforts of Mr. Thomas Rivers that this branch of modern fruit culture has made such rapid progress during the last thirty years … Pot trees … require much attention in watering … By purchasing them established in pots and well set with flower-buds at least one year's start is gained over trees dug up and newly potted.

Should you decide to use your conservatory as an orchard house, it would be particularly suitable for the dry, warm needs of citrus. By Rivers' time citrus fruit had long been planted in large containers so that they could be moved seasonally and Rivers exported orange trees worldwide from Sawbridgeworth, including 'Valencia Late' to California for commercial production, as Florida varieties proved unsuitable. On a domestic scale he perfected growing fruit trees in containers for all gardeners. Two outstanding large-scale examples of containerized fruit culture can be seen in the restored orchard houses at Audley End in Essex and Cragside in Northumberland based on his plans.

Jane Loudon in *The Amateur Gardener* says:

> ... [pots of] the more tender kind of greenhouse plants ... particularly the orange and lemon trees and all kinds of succulent plants ... infested with insects should be washed with a sponge, and if a hardwooded plant, the stem should be brushed; and then, the pot being laid on its side, the plant should be well syringed on the under side of its leaves; first, with cold water, and if that does not prove sufficient, with water heated to 140°–150°F, which Mr. Barnes, the late gardener at Bicton, assures us is sufficient to destroy the mealy bug, coccus, or any other kind of insect which infests ...

She explains how Mr Barnes proposed to lay the plant on its side:

> Mr. Barnes's plan is, first, to provide a piece of cloth, cut in a circular form, a little larger than the pots, and with a slit or opening halfway across it to admit the stem of the plant ... A broad hem or string case must be made round the circumference of the cloth, in which a string must be inserted, so as to draw and tie round under the rim of the pot. A good handful of moss should be put 'underneath the cloth, so as to keep all tight together, and prevent the earth from falling out and the hot water from getting to the roots of the plants', etc. Two bricks should be then provided and the rim of the pot rested upon them ...

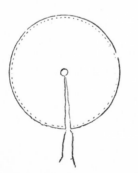

Mrs Loudon recommended sealing large pots with a cloth before leaning them against two bricks for a thorough syringing with hot water to kill insects.

SECOND QUALITY GARDEN SYRINGES.

No.2. No.1.No.3. No.4. No.9. No. 5. No. 6. No.7. No. 8.

No. 1.—Ladies' Syringe, with Jet only, 12-in. barrel 4/3
No. 2.—Ladies' Syringe, with Rose and Jet, 12-in. barrel   ...   4/9
No. 3.—Ladies' Syringe, with two Roses and Jet, 12-in. barrel   6/8
No. 4.—Middle Size, with two Roses and Jet, 16-in. barrel ...   9/0
No. 5.—Full size, with two Roses and Jet, 18-in. barrel   ...   11/0
No. 6.—Full size, 18-in. barrel, improved Rose 12/3
No. 7.—Full size, 18-in. barrel, Ball Valve 13/3
No. 8.—18-in. barrel, Patent Ball Valve 14/9
No. 9.—Knuckle-jointed, 19-in. barrel 17/6

'so as to admit of the plant being raised or lowered in an oblique direction without touching the ground; this will also admit of turning the plant round at pleasure, so as to allow of syringing every part of the plant, as well over the surface of the leaves and heads of flowers, as on the under side of them, so that hot water may touch every part of the plant except the roots'.   It must be observed, that the plant must be syringed, and not watered ... while water ... would scald the leaves if poured upon them in a continuous stream from a watering pot.

This is a good tip not only for insect eradication but also for general transportation of potted plants by car or barrow.

Vines

The Book of Genesis describes some of the earliest vines, and how after the Flood, *c.* 5000 BC, 'Noah began to be an husbandman, and he planted a vineyard And he drank of the wine, and was drunken.' Later the Romans, having learnt much from the ancient Egyptians, became great vine growers, as well as grape eaters and wine makers. Plant names often celebrate their history, and today the Roman name *vitis* survives as the vine's genus name, and the large white grape 'Muscat of Alexandria', which requires warmth and hand pollination, recalls the ancient vines grown on the Nile Delta. The planting of wine grapes outside Italy was strictly forbidden until *c.* AD 280, when the Emperor Probus ordered his troops to create vineyards wherever they were stationed, in order to prevent idleness.

Pliny has plenty of advice for first-century viticulturists in his *Naturalis Historia*: '... he set in hand to husband and manure them ... for he makes fallows of his wine-plots anew, and delveth them all over again ... but what with digging, stirring and meddling therewith ... he brought his vineyards

ABOVE *Like so many Victorian and Edwardian tools, syringes came in a multiplicity of sizes.*

to so good a pass within one eight years.' He notes that 'the radish and the laurel do harm to the vine'. Could this be because the radish attracts flea beetles and the laurel or sweet bay casts too much shade? Vines need to be grown in full sun in well-drained soil and kept weed free. It is said that they benefit from being underplanted with hyssop.

Gerard reports in his *Herball* of 1597 that 'Columella saith Vines must be pruned before the yong branches spring forth. Palladius writeth, in Februarie: if they be pruned later they lose their nourishment with weeping.' In England you can prune a vine until March but after that the sap run is such that pruning would be detrimental to the vine's welfare.

Pliny suggests that we are not alone in needing a break from our routines to get back into shape: 'The Importance of Holidays. Over and besides, the manner is otherwhiles to untie the vine, and for certain days together to give it liberty for to wander loosely, and to spread itself out of order, yea, and to lie at ease along the ground.' Anyone trying to prune a vine wound around a pergola or frame might well contemplate unwinding the vine and giving it a holiday before pruning and tying it back. This way you can assess what needs pruning branch by branch more easily than through a mesh of branches and thus avoid inadvertently cutting off your best branch. Wait until the day has warmed up when the branches are more flexible and less brittle and liable to break.

The vine supports C.D. Warner's belief 'in the intellectual, if not the moral, qualities of vegetables', as he explains in *My Summer in a Garden* (1918):

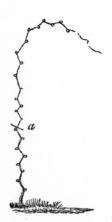

There was a worthless vine that (or who) started up midway between a grape-trellis and a row of bean-poles, some three feet from each, but a little nearer the trellis. When it came out of the ground, it looked round to see what it should do. The trellis was already occupied. The bean-pole was empty. There was evidently a little – the best – chance of light, air, and sole proprietorship on the pole. And the vine started for the pole, and began to climb it

In The English Gardener *Cobbett recommends cutting a vine whip back to eight buds before training along a trellis of three rows at 16-foot (5-metre) centres. Tidy and fruitful.*

with determination. Here was as distinct an act of choice, of reason, as a boy exercises when he goes into a forest, and, looking about, decides which tree he will climb. And, besides, how did the vine know enough to travel in exactly the right direction, three feet, to find what it wanted? This is intellect.

Samuel Wood gives dogmatic instructions in *The Tree Planter, Propagator and Pruner*, published in 1894. 'Now that glass is so cheap there seems but little reason for growing grapes out of doors; yet as it is not at present within the reach of many who like a bunch of grapes, and who grow them on the walls of the house, some practical advice as to the management of the vine may be useful ... whenever a Vine ... gets into a worn out state so far as fruiting goes ... there is but one remedy ... cut it clean back ... No half doing things of this sort will suffice.' Don't forget, though, to do it before March.

Perhaps it was lack of such firm action that contributed to the failure of the vines at 5 Cheyne Row, Chelsea, the house into which Thomas Carlyle moved in May 1834. His wife, Jane, wrote to her family: 'Behind we have a garden (so called in the language of flattery) in the worst of order, but boasting of two vines which produced two bunches of grapes in the season which "might be eaten", and a walnut tree, from which I gathered almost sixpence worth of Walnuts.'

Soft fruits

An anonymous writer who wished to ensure that those growing melons enjoyed the fruits of their labour at the point of perfection writes in 1699:

> Every gardner nowadays knows how to raise melons, but few to govern them; when you would gather a ripe melon, you will notice its turning a little yellow, for that time it does ordinarily ripen ... the gardner must therefore not fail of visiting the Meloniere at the least three times a day, for this critical time. After twenty-four hours' keeping; for Contrary to the Vulgar Opinion, it should be preserved in some sweet dry place and not eaten immediately it comes from the garden. A perfect Transcendent Melon will be Full, Juicy, and without vacuity.

C.D. Warner would have agreed with the quest to enjoy fruit 'without vacuity'. In *My Summer in a Garden* he compares the empty-flavoured cucumber unfavourably with the melon: 'Then there is the cool cucumber, like so many people – good for nothing when it is ripe and the mildness gone out of it. How inferior in quality it is to the melon, which [i.e. the cucumber] grows upon a similar vine, is of a like watery consistency, but is not half so valuable. The cucumber is a sort of low comedian in a company where the melon is a minor gentleman.'

CURRANTS
C.D. Warner is more positive about berries. 'They live in another and more ideal region, except, perhaps, the currants. Here we see that, even among berries, there are degrees of breeding. The currant is well enough, clear as truth, and excellent in colour; but I ask you to notice how far it is from the exclusive hauteur of the aristocratic strawberry, and the native refinement of the quietly elegant raspberry.'

Philip Miller offers a guide to eighteenth-century currants in his *Gardener's Dictionary* (1731):

RIBES, The Curran-tree ... Common red ..., large Dutch red ..., Common white ..., Large Dutch white ..., The Champagne ... Sorts are preserved in all curious Gardens for the sake of their Fruits: indeed of late Years, the common red and white Currans have become plenty in England these producing much larger and fairer Fruit to the Sight than the common sorts, though I think the common Sorts are much better flavoured ... The black Curran ... is preserved in some old Gardens; but the Fruit having a disagreeable strong Taste, has occasioned its being but little cultivated of late Years ... The American black Curran was obtained by Mr. Peter Collinson from America ... The Manner of this Plant's Flowering is very different ... but the Fruit being somewhat like our black Curran, is not much esteemed ... These plants produce their Fruit upon the former Year's Wood, and also upon small Snags [spurs] which come out of the old Wood; so that, in pruning them, these Snags should be preserved.

Cobbett tells us in *The English Gardener* (1829) that 'the finest currants are those which grow rather in the shade; the fruit becomes larger there, and has not the disagreeable tartness which it acquires if ripened in a hot sun. This shrub flourishes and bears well under the shade of other trees. There are three sorts of currants, distinguished by their different colours of red, white and black, and the several uses of all these are too well known to need my description.'

On pruning, he says:

When the young currant-tree is planted out, it ought not to be suffered to have any limbs within five or six inches of the ground ... When the limbs come out, or rather the shoots that are to become limbs, there should not be more than four or six suffered to go on as principal limbs. By shortening the shoots at the end of the first year, you double the number of limbs. These, as in the case of the espalier apple-tree, are to be kept constantly clear of side-shoots by cutting off, every winter, the last summer's wood within one bud or so of the limb; and when the limbs have attained their proper length, the shoot at the end of each limb should also be annually cut off, so that the tree, when it has received its pruning, consists of a certain number of limbs, looking like so many rugged sticks with bunches of spurs sticking out of them ... On these spurs come the fruit in quantities prodigious.

If you are faced with geriatric currant bushes Jane Loudon's advice in *The Amateur Gardener* might help: 'Old currant bushes have a wonderful amount of vitality, and the stock may often be renewed or increased by dividing the bushes when they have formed a broad stool of roots. The main limbs may be pulled away separately with roots attached and if planted in good rich soil, will form good bushes quickly, and bear good crops of fruit. This plan is advisable in emergencies; but young plants make the finest and healthiest bushes in the end, and a young stock from cuttings should therefore be raised occasionally.'

Blackcurrants, she says, 'bear in the same way as the red, but they do not bear cutting back, and should only be freely thinned; the more young shoots that can be left the better, if they are not crowded.' Of redcurrants she simply writes: 'Red currants .. require nearly the same treatment as gooseberries.' Cobbett, too, says in *The English Gardener*: 'Gooseberries are propagated, planted out, trained, and pruned, in precisely the same manner as directed for currants.'

GOOSEBERRIES

Traditionally, gooseberries are first eaten seven weeks after Easter on Whit Sunday, which is surprising, as this is a moveable feast. If Easter falls early the elder tree flowers at the same time and the muscat flavour of its flowers balanced with the tartness of gooseberries makes an excellent combination.

Sam Beeton in his *New Dictionary of Every-Day Gardening* (1862) sounds a warning over predatory gooseberry caterpillars: 'The bushes should be carefully looked over once a week to watch the hatching of the eggs when the infected leaves may be picked off. To prevent the fly from settling, the bushes should be dusted over with hellebore powder, or watered with a strong decoction of the Digitalis, or common foxglove. If the caterpillar has begun its ravages, the ground beneath the bush should sprinkled with new lime, and a double barrelled gun fired two or three times under it to shake the caterpillars down into it' – a tip best left in the archives.

Throughout *The Gardener's Dictionary* Philip Miller guides the gardener's cutting hand, and on gooseberries he says: 'In the pruning of these Shrubs, most People make use of Gardensheers, observing only to cut the Head round ... whereby the Branches become so much crouded, that what Fruit is produced, never grow to half the Size as it would do, were the Branches thinned and pruned according to Art; which should always be done with a pruning Knife ... It is common Practice with the Gardeners near London ... to prune them soon after Michaelmas, and then to dig up the Ground between the Rows, and plant it with Coleworts for Spring-use ... a Piece of Husbandry well worth practising ... where Persons are confined for Room.' Standard mop-headed gooseberries have come back into fashion and would look extremely ornamental underplanted with red cabbages.

RASPBERRIES

How about our native fruit, the 'quietly elegant raspberry'? Gerard was not enthusiastic, describing 'The Raspis or Framboise' as 'in taste not very pleasant'. By the nineteenth century raspberries were much improved, and in 1823 the Horticultural Society of London was able to report that there were twenty-three varieties available. William Robinson writes in the foreword to the fifteenth edition (1933) of *The English Flower Garden*: 'The greatest improvement of all fruit in our days is that of the native Raspberry. It varies much in cultivation, and from seedlings we have often got several

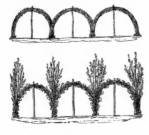

good and late kinds ... The Raspberry is quite free of acid and easy of cultivation. Markham [Robinson's head gardener and a clematis specialist and enthusiast] takes much interest in it and grows it very well, supplying us the whole summer, right into November, with delicious fruit.'

Cobbett, who devotes about a third of *The English Gardener* to fruits in alphabetical order, describes how to cultivate the raspberry:

The stems of raspberries should be prevented from bending down, when loaded with leaves and with fruit, by stakes put along the sides of the rows, and by little rods tied to these stakes. Every stool will send out, during summer, a great number of shoots. When the leaf is down, these should be all taken away, except about four to produce fruit the next year. The shoots that have borne during the summer, die in the autumn; these should also be removed; and, in November, and again in March, all the ground should be well and truly digged; and the weeds should be kept down completely during the whole of the summer. One manuring in three years will be sufficient. The common little raspberry is but a poorish thing; and every one should take care to have the Antwerp if possible. Raspberries, when gathered ... are a very delicious fruit.

'Antwerp' was one of the yellow and white varieties introduced from Antwerp, of which 'Yellow Antwerp' is still grown. Sadly the varieties Robinson grew – he says: 'The best kinds we grow are – Ameloire de Congy, Perpetual Superlative, Perpetual Superlative Yellow, Surprise of Autumn and Merveille des Quatre Saissons' – are seemingly now lost to cultivation.

Judge J.H. Logan of Santa Cruz, California experimented with crossing a wild blackberry with a red raspberry and in 1881 the vigorous and aromatic loganberry was introduced.

ABOVE *How might the Edwardian gardener like her raspberries trained? Regular style on two wires or fashioned into ornamental arches?*

STRAWBERRIES

Cobbett has much to say in *The English Gardener* on the strawberry. 'This is a fruit, exceeded in no one respect (except that of keeping) but by very few; and surpassing a very great majority of the fruits of this country. It is so well known, that to describe either plant or fruit would be almost an insult to the reader ... To cultivate strawberries in beds, suffering them to cover the whole of the ground with their runners and young plants, is a miserable method, proceeding from the suggestions either of idleness or of greediness, and sure to lead to the defeating the object of this latter. Strawberries will bear a little in this way, though not much; but the fruit will be of small and insipid flavour.'

Instead he advises this method: 'The runners begin to start usually in May, not making much progress at first, on account of the coldish weather; but, by the middle of June, the runners have produced an abundance of plants. You take the earliest and stoutest of these, plant them out before the end of the first week in August, and these plants will bear abundantly the next year. Great care must be taken in this planting. The ground should be made rich and fine: the root is but small, and the weather is hot; therefore, the root should be fixed well in the ground with the fingers; and a little rain or pond water should be given to the plants. They should be attended to very carefully to see that worms do not rear them out of the ground or move them at all ... By November, the plants will be stout: ... and, in the month of June, ... they will produce a crop worth fifty times the labour bestowed upon them.' You could also pot some up and bring them on under glass for an early crop. Strawberries thrive on rich soil and under dappled shade. If you are already growing cultivated or ornamental strawberries, it is worth taking their offsets and regularly refreshing your stocks.

Cobbett continues: 'Before I come to speak of the different sorts let me notice three things: preserving strawberries from the birds and slugs; keeping them from being covered with dirt by the heavy rains; and giving them water if the ground be at all dry. As to the first of these, the wood-pigeons, the common pigeons, the doves, the blackbirds, the jack-daws, the thrushes, and even some of the small birds, invade the strawberry clumps, and, if unresisted destroy a great part of the fruit ... nothing is a protection but a net ... The slug is a still more bitter enemy; and, in some seasons, where strawberries are suffered to run together in beds, more than half the fruit is consumed or spoiled by these nasty and mischievous reptiles. The remedy is, to examine the clumps well just as the strawberries are beginning to be ripe. See that there are no slugs about the stems of the leaves, and then make a little circle of hot lime, at half a foot or so at the extremity of the leaves of the clumps. No slug will enter that magic circle.' Today some commercial strawberry growers import hedgehogs, who relish a protein rich diet of slugs.

Cobbett again: 'The other precaution; namely, to keep the fruit from being beaten by the rain down amongst the dirt, short grass-mowings, or moss, the latter being the best of the two, should be laid round the stems of the plants, just as the fruit begins to ripen. This will completely guard against the evil: come what rain will, the fruit will always be clean. The last thing that I have to mention, is the watering; and a real good watering with rain-water, or pond-water, should be given just when the blossoms are falling and fruit begins to set. Blacking the ground over with the rose of the watering-pot is of no use at all; the water should be poured out of the nose of the pot, held close down to the plant; and one gallon of water, at least, should be given at one time to every clump of plants.' In other words, get the water to the roots, thereby keeping the fruit dry – remember how quickly strawberries rot when there is high rainfall at the fruiting stage.0

Cobbett goes on: 'As to the sorts of the strawberries, the scarlet is the earliest; … the hautbois … the Kew Pine, the Chili, the White Alpine and the Red Alpine; which two latter are vulgarly called wood strawberries. The hautboy has a musky and singular flavour as well as smell, and some people prefer it to all others. But the great strawberry of all, now-a-days, is that which was some years ago raised from seed by Mr. KEEN [sic] of Islington, which is therefore called the KEEN's seedling; and this strawberry, which is the only one used for forcing in the King's gardens, has nearly supplanted every other sort. It is early; it is a prodigious bearer; the fruit is large, and very large; and it surpasses, in my opinion, all others in flavour.'

A vote of thanks should be raised to nurseryman Michael Keens. The native European strawberry (*Fragaria vesca*) was gathered from woodlands and transplanted into gardens long before Thomas Tusser advocated doing so in the sixteenth century. In the early seventeenth century Tradescant the Younger enthused about the recent introduction of the bland but large *F. virginiana* from eastern North America. In the eighteenth century three other varieties were then domesticated: the alpine *F. vesca semperflorens*, the red-and-white fruited hautbois (*F. moschata*) and *F. viridis*. In 1714 six female plants of *F. chiloensis*, which grows along the Pacific American coast from Alaska to Chile, arrived in France. A.W. Duchesne crossed them with the Virginian strawberry to obtain what he described as the 'pineapple strawberry', but his work was lost in the maelstrom of the 1789 French Revolution. Enter Mr Keens, who introduced 'Keen's Imperial' in 1814, and seven years later 'Keen's Seedling', the large tasty strawberry described by Cobbett. By 1892 Laxton Brothers had introduced the delicious 'Royal Sovereign', still available but sadly susceptible to disease; 'Cambridge Late Pine' and 'Mara des Bois' are also still available and the white fruiting alpines taste like white chocolate.

In his foreword to *The English Flower Garden* Robinson shows no enthusiasm for Cobbett's 'Chili' strawberry: 'Strawberries are a failure with us. Sir Henry Thompson, the surgeon, said to me that the worst thing he knew to create acid in the blood was the common Strawberry of the London market. It is not a British plant, but a Chilean one.'

On the other hand, Henry A. Bright is enthusiastic about the hautbois (*Fragaria moschata*), writing in *A Year in a Lancashire Garden* (1901):

> I am trying, too, for the first time, to grow Hautbois Strawberries, which are almost unknown with us ... A year or two ago I was breakfasting with a well-known and most courtly physician ... A dish of beautiful Hautbois was on the table ... 'Yes' said our host, 'they are now getting very rare. Sometimes a patient says to me, "May I not have a little fruit?" "Certainly not!" is my answer. "Surely a few Strawberries?" Then, that I may not seem a great curmudgeon, I say, "Well, a few Strawberries, but be sure they are Hautbois;" and I know they can't get them!' To ordinary Strawberries a Hautbois is what a Tea Rose is to ordinary Roses.

For an ornamental effect, grow pink-flowered or variegated-leaved strawberries. Tusser's recommended combination in *Five Hundred Points of Good Husbandry* (1573),

> The gooseberry, raspberry and roses all three,
> With strawberries under them, trimly agree,

was probably effective, as gooseberries, raspberries and many roses like a good mulch of manure, and strawberries thrive on rich soil under dappled shade.

VACCINIUM

Gerard describes in his *Herball* (1597) a plant that was enjoyed in much the same way as strawberries:

> The people of Cheshire do eat the blacke Wortles in creame and milke, as in these South parts we eate Strawberries. The Red Wortle is not of such a pleasant taste as the blacke, and therefore not so much used to be eaten; but … they make the fairest carnation colour in the World. He explains that Wortle berries or Vaccinia, or Worts … differ from Violets, neither are they esteemed for their floures but berries: of these Worts there be divers sorts found out by the later Writers. Vaccinia nigra … is a base and low shrub or wooddy plant … not much unlike the leaves of Box or the Myrtle tree … These plants prosper best in a leane barren soile, and in untoiled wooddy places: they are now and then found on high hills subject to the winde, and upon mountaines: they grow plentifully … in Middlesex on Hampsted heath…. in Cheshire called Broxen hills neere Beeston castle … and in the wood by Highgate called Finchley wood … The Wortle berries do floure in May, and their fruit is ripe in June.

Pliny and Virgil also describe *Vaccinium*, now the name of a genus which encompasses blueberries, bilberries and whortleberries. If you cannot pick them from the wild and decide to grow any of these you will need very acid soil, 'subject to the winde', as Gerard says, because they need good air circulation to allow frosty air to drain away easily but not unduly strong winds.

Roots, greens and corn

HERBES AND ROOTES TO BOILE OR TO BUTTER
Beanes set in winter
Cabbegis, sowe in March and after remoove
Carrets
Citrons, sowe in May
Navewes sowe in June.
Pompions in May.
Perseneps in winter.

Thomas Tusser, *Five Hundred Points of Good Husbandry* (1573)

In his *Encyclopaedia of Cottage, Farm and Villa Architecture and Furniture* of 1833, John Loudon expresses the opinion that 'The grand drawback to every kind of improvement is the vulgar and degrading idea that certain things are beyond our reach.' As an encouragement to his readers he invited young architects amongst his readers, who were better off than Cobbett's rural cottagers, to design ideal cottages and gardens with at least 40 square rods (¼ acre/0.1012 hectares) for a self-sufficient plot. Loudon's own recommendations are the staples of any vegetable garden: '1 rod onions and leeks; ½ rod carrots; ½ rod Windsor beans; 1 rod parsnips; 3 rods cabbages with a row of scarlet runners to be planted around the edges, to give a yield of 525 cabbages; 4 rods early potatoes; 4 rods Prussian potatoes; 6 rods Devonshire potatoes as well as a pig, fowls and ducks and if space allowed radishes, early peas, beans, cos lettuce, barley, leeks and cucumber and tobacco' – all grown in sizeable quantitites.

Jane Loudon in *The Amateur Gardener* allows for more individuality and a bigger range of vegetables. She omits barley and tobacco and includes brassica sowings that are modest by comparison with her husband's gargantuan cabbage proposals, saying: 'Cabbage, Cauliflowers, Savoys, and all the brassicas should be got in packets, as a very small quantity of seed will raise enough … indeed, it is advisable to get the plants from the nursery

ABOVE *Taken c. 1910 by Minnis of Highbury, Hitchin. The poses and setting exemplify the traditional roles of the man providing vegetables, grown, harvested and cleaned, for his lady to demonstrate her culinary skills.*

or from some obliging friend, and so save a great amount of worry.' Dear reader, I trust you have not had sleepless nights worrying about cabbage seedlings, but it is certainly easier to buy plants of your favourite varieties. Jane recommends 'Little Pixie, small, but of the finest quality; and, if planted close, will yield more for the table than the large-growing kinds, many of which we consider unfit for the table at all.' Likewise her general advice on quantities is more cautious than her husband's, allowing for individual needs. 'In giving directions for choosing seeds the general rule is to say how much of this, that, and the other thing will be required for a quarter of an acre ... Such advice only serves to puzzle. The fact is, no two individuals' wants are the same ... What I propose is, to give as near as possible the amount of space required for a given quantity of seed, and by this means each person will be enabled to calculate to a nicety the seed required for his own individual wants ... A mere pinch of Celery will raise hundreds of plants.'

QUALITY BEFORE SIZE
'All who have gardens should fight against the deterioration of some of our best vegetables through the mania for size. Although the flavour of vegetables may not be so obvious as of fruit, it is often their essential

ABOVE *A postcard posted in Jarrow on 31 December 1904, inscribed: 'This is the house Jack Built not the one in the Nursery Rhyme. But the house that he built to nurse Plants in. In which you will have enough to do.' Seemingly heated, judging by the stove pipe.*

quality. A change in size, by adding to the watery tissue of the plant, may destroy the flavour, and doubling or trebling the size of the article itself, as has been done in the case of Brussels Sprout, which is no longer the same little rosette of green but a coarse Cabbage sprout. Bad, too, is the raising of new varieties lacking in flavour, and abolishing old kinds, from supposed deficiency in size.' Not a modern argument for heritage and heirloom seeds but William Robinson writing in *The Vegetable Garden* in 1905. We are enjoying a revival in the quest for taste rather than quantity.

ONIONS

If growing onions and leeks, you could follow Pliny's advice in his *Naturalis Historia*: '… if you would have garlic, onions and such like, not to smell strong and stink so as they do, the common opinion and rule is, that they should not be set or sown but when the moon is under the earth, nor yet be gathered and taken up but in her conjunction with sun.' Garlic was introduced throughout Europe by the Romans as part of the army's *materia medica*. Remember to divide the bulb into cloves before planting. One saying about garlic advises 'Plant on the shortest day, harvest on the longest'; however, fifteenth-century John the Gardener recommends sowing onions, garlic and leeks on St Valentine's day. Gerard in his 1597 *Herball* suggests 'sowing onions … many times mixed with other herbs, as with Lettuce, Parseneps, and Carrets … sowne with Savorie … it prospereth better'.

Miss Mitford, who charted the lives and habits of her fellow villagers in *Our Village* (1824), describes one of her neighbours' ways of looking after onions: 'Dame Simmons makes an original use of her pond, most ingeniously watering her onion-bed with a new mop – now a dip, and now a twirl … It is as good an imitation of a shower as one should wish to see in a summer day. A squirt is nothing to it.'

CARROTS

There is a grain of truth in the advice that eating carrots enables you to see in the dark, as modern research has shown that the vitamin A in them strengthens eyesight. It is also more assimilable after cooking than when eaten raw. But does Bugs Bunny know something we don't? Other unattributed sources claim that eating raw carrots enables true lovers to see one another without inhibition, so could the carrot be related to Pliny's erythaicon: '… the root is hard and white within, the rind whereof is red, and in taste is somewhat sweetish: an herb ordinarily found (as they say) upon mountains: … the root is of that virtue, that if it be held only in a man's hand, it will cause the flesh to rise and incite him to the company of women.'

By 1600 in the Netherlands yellow and orange carrots were available, and they were among the first seeds carried by settlers to the Americas. Poorer settlers hid essential seeds in the hems of their women's dresses to avoid theft. A traditional requirement was quantity, and poorer people grew mammoth roots that needed long slow cooking – carrots that survive today in the produce show's 'longest root' section. The more refined palates of the well-fed classes demanded sweeter, tender, orange, finger-like varieties. As late as 1913 seed suppliers Suttons & Sons of Reading note in *The Culture of Vegetables and Flowers*: 'Turning to the fine art department, the Forcing French Horn Carrot demands attention as an elegant and delicate root that appears on tables where cottagers' Carrots dare not be seen.'

Philip Miller lists five species of carrot, including 'two commonly cultivated in Gardens for the Kitchen': '*Daucus sativus, radice atrorubente*', the dark red-rooted garden carrot, and '*Daucus sativus, radice aurantii coloris*', the orange red carrot. He reckons that the deepest-coloured are the most esteemed and '*Daucus sativus, radice alba* … the White is generally preferred as the sweetest.'

Thomas Jefferson grew numerous varieties as field and garden crops in his garden at Monticello near Charlottesville in Virginia and his favourites were 'Early Scarlet' and 'Long Orange'.

Jane Loudon includes a monthly seed guide, of which she says: 'I have carefully avoided anything savouring of novelty which has not been found equal or superior to older varieties … very meritorious novelties are occasionally introduced … I range the names according to their earliness.' The carrots she recommends include: 'Sutton's Champion Short Horn, James' Intermediate, and Altringham; the Short Horn for earliest, and the Intermediate for shallow soils'. Of 'Sutton's Champion Short Horn', Suttons & Sons say: 'On heavy lumpy land long clean roots cannot be

Orange Belgian, or Long Orange Green-top, carrot – very hardy and productive.

secured by any kind of tillage. But for these unsuitable soils we have …
Sutton's Champion Short Horn … which requires no great depth of earth
… they make an elegant and delicate dish.'

While he was editing *The Garden* magazine, popularizing the water lilies
of French nurseryman Joseph Bory Latour-Marliac and gardening his own
extensive garden at Gravetye Manor in Sussex, William Robinson edited *The
Vegetable Garden: Illustrations, Descriptions, and Culture of the Garden Vegetables of
Cold and Temperate Climates* by the great French nurseryman Vilmorin-
Andrieux, published in 1885. In this, Vilmorin-Andrieux describes the
following varieties, all of which are still available today:

Flanders or Sandwich Formerly quantities of it were sent to the Paris
market from Flanders in waggons at the close of winter, when the Scarlet
Horn and the Long Red Carrots were beginning to grow scarce. It is now
less frequently seen there since the Parisian cultivators discovered that by
successional sowings fresh Carrots can be raised at all seasons.

St. Valery A large handsome variety, the connecting-link between
Half-long and Long varieties of Red Carrot. The root, which is very
straight, very smooth, and bright red, is very broad at the neck, where
it is frequently 2 to 3 in. in diameter, so that the entire length, which
may be 10 to 12 in., is only about four times the diameter, which would
almost bring it into the category of the Half-long varieties. It is
suitable for field culture, but does best in light, rich, well-dug soil. The
leaves are remarkably slight for the size of the root. This fine variety
was for a long time grown only in its native locality, but since it became
better known it has grown in favour for, with a handsome appearance
and good quality, it is a good kitchen-garden as well as a good field
Carrot, combining great productiveness with a fine regular shape and
thick, sweet, tender flesh.

James' Intermediate Carrot This variety is evidently an improved
form of the Half-long Scarlet Carrot, but as it has now been a good
while in very general cultivation, it has undergone a considerable
amount of modification, in consequence of which it exhibits …
diversities of character in different districts. In a general way it may be
described as a handsome Half-long Carrot, with a long, pointed, well-
coloured root, vigorous and rapid in growth, and having a stoutish
neck, as might be expected from a variety which is as much grown in

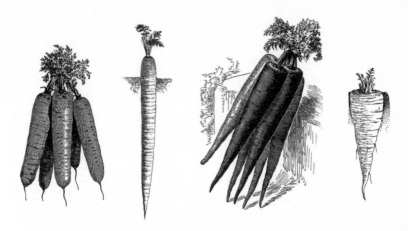

fields as in gardens. It is very productive …

Altringham Carrot This variety, which is of English origin, has been for a long time known and valued in France. It is a very long, slender kind, with the flesh entirely red … and of excellent quality … Of late years the English growers have considerably altered the characteristics of their Altringham Carrot … the new form is much thicker, shorter, and smoother. This is an improvement, as it makes the lifting of roots much easier.

Today there are many more varieties: my 1995 edition of *The Fruit and Vegetable Finder* lists 179 carrot varieties whose names range alphabetically from 'Allegro' to 'Yslanda', in some cases echoing their origins and size – the varieties 'Amsterdam Forcing 3 Sweetheart', 'Nantes Champion Scarlet Horn' and 'St Valery', for instance, recall their arrival in England in the sixteenth century with north European immigrants. The white carrot 'White Fodder' is now enjoying a renaissance as a designer vegetable with the added bonus of being ideal for those allergic to carotene.

Raising carrots from seed to match their catalogue descriptions requires skill. Philip Miller writes: 'the Seeds are hairy, and in Shape of lice'. This hirsute quality makes sowing carrot seeds evenly difficult, and combating the hairiness attracts a range of advice. He continues: '… you should therefore rub it well through both Hands, whereby the Seed will be separated before

ABOVE *Gorgeous carrots from William Robinson's* The Vegetable Garden: *Red Long Smooth Meaux carrot; Altringham; Long Blood-red carrot; Flanders or Sandwich carrot.*

it is sown: then you should chuse a calm Day to sow it; for if the Wind blows, it will be impossible to sow it equal; for the Seeds, being very light, will be blown into Heaps: when the Seed is sown, you should tread the Ground pretty close with your Feet, that it may be buried; and then rake the Ground level.' Separating the seeds is essential to ensure that the roots develop well and avoiding a windy day is common sense but although light treading stops the anchor root from exploring any further whilst the plant's first leaves establish you should do so with caution. Sam Beeton in his *New Dictionary of Every-Day Gardening* gives better advice: '... for the purpose of separating it, [carrot seed should] be rubbed up in a peck or so of tolerably dry soil, which will help to bury it when sown, using the rake to press it in.' Mixing small seeds with dry soil is an excellent idea and a rake is better than a boot, leaving the soil open enough for the root to develop.

Miller's observation that carrots 'delight in a warm sandy Soil ... and should be dug pretty deep, that the Roots may the better run down' is spot on. This is because 'if they meet with any Obstruction, they are very apt to grow forked, and shoot out lateral Roots, especially where the Ground is too much dunged ... which will also occasion their being worm-eaten'. Harry A. Day endorses Miller's advice in *Your Kitchen Garden* (1935): '... although the stump-rooted varieties will flourish on soil of medium depth ... No fresh, rank, or strong manure should be put into the upper layer of soil, but deep down, with the subsoil.' Stones, too, can deform.

Beeton cannot resist the temptation of producing a behemoth root. 'To produce carrots and parsnips of an extraordinary size, make a very deep hole with a long dibble; ram the earth well round it while the dibble is in, and when it is removed, fill up the hole with fine rich earth. Sow a few seeds on the top ... and when up, draw out all except the one plant nearest to the centre of the hole. Prodigious carrots and parsnips may be produced by this means.' Exhibition root growers today use drainpipes similarly so that the carrot can enjoy a trouble-free run.

On the question of when to sow, in *The Gardener's Labyrinth* (1577) Thomas Hill includes carrots among seeds 'that at the will of the Gardener may be committed to the earth, either in Harvest, or Spring time ... under a gentle aire, and in a battle ground'.

Miller says: 'The first Season for sowing the Seeds is soon after Christmas, if the weather is open, which should be in warm Borders, under Walls, Pales, or Hedges, tho' they should not be sown immediately close thereto; … In July you may sow again, to stand the Winter; by which Method you will have early Carrots in March, before the Spring-sowing will be fit to draw; but these are seldom so well tasted, and are often very rough and sticky.' In *Vegetables for Home and Exhibition* (1927) Edwin Bennett comments: 'Young, quickly grown specimens ought to receive more attention than is generally given them. By this I mean that frequent sowings should be made from the commencement of the New Year until the last week in August, especially in large gardens, the earliest and latest sowings being made under glass.' Both pieces of advice reflect the fact that although carrots are a cool-season crop, if temperatures consistently drop below 16°C (60°F) they become pale, long and tapered – so unless you have a heated greenhouse, it is best to wait for early spring. Note too, that if sown in July, they may have to make their prime growth in temperatures above 28°C (84°F), which reduces their top growth and, as Miller says, the roots become very strongly flavoured – but are likely to avoid infestation by carrot flies. How quick is *quickly grown*? In the region of fourteen weeks.

In 1664 Stephen Blake advises: 'That you let them not grow too thick [densely] … the best way to prevent this, is to hoe them ass our London Gardeners do, so that each Carrot stand ten inches one from another, or thereabouts.' Miller recommends: 'When the Plants are come up, you should hoe the Ground with a small Hoe about three Inches wide, cutting down all the young weeds, and separating the Plants to four Inches Distance each Way, that they may get Strength; and in about three Weeks after … hoe the Ground over a second time, in which you should be careful not to leave two Carrots close to each other, … cutting down all Weeds, and slightly stirring the Surface of the Ground in every Place, the better to prevent young Weeds from springing, as also to facilitate the Growth of the young Carrots … three Weeks or a Month after, you must hoe them a third time, when you must clear the Weeds … cut out the Carrots to the Distance they are to remain.' Such constant hoeing could also disturb the larvae of the devastating carrot fly, hatching from eggs carefully placed near the roots for ready burrowing. And undoubtedly carrots kept weed free will grow better roots and provide higher yields. Today for large carrots the recommendation is 40 plants per square yard (50 per square metre) with 2 inches (5 cm) between plants and 12 inches (30 cm) between rows; and for small carrots 130 per square yard (165 per square metre).

Suttons & Sons describe the warning signs of the carrot fly: 'The presence of the larvae in the tap-root is made known by the change in the colour of the leaves from green to yellow. The plant should be immediately taken up, and the grubs destroyed by dipping the Carrots in hot water.' Carrot fly, which also attacks parsnips, can detect the merest waft of carrot roots, so how can you disguise the scent? Miller writes:

> Many People mix several other Sorts of Seeds, as Leek, Onion, Parsnep, Radish, etc. amongst their Carrots; and others plant Beans, etc, but, in my Opinion, neither of these Methods is good … and besides, it is not only more sightly, but better for the Plants of each Kind to be sown separate … but when three or four Kinds are mixed together, the Ground is seldom at Liberty before the succeeding Spring: besides, where Beans, or any other tall-growing Plants, are mixed or planted amongst the Carrots, it is apt to make them grow more in Top than Root, so that they will not be half so large as if sown singly, without any other Plants amongst them.

True, but scatter-sowing coriander and chervil with the carrot seed may help to deter the carrot fly and you can pick coriander and chervil leaves until you harvest the carrots.

To avoid other pests, if you have an open fire or a supply of lime or guano (droppings from sea birds), you could take the following advice from Suttons & Sons: 'A good dressing of soot given to all land devoted to Carrots will always prove beneficial, and soot and guano may be applied during showery weather around the young plants. Carrots [and parsnips] are the prey especially of the wireworm, slug, and leather-jacket; and the maggot is often destructive. These may be combated … by the use of wood ashes, lime, and soot upon the soil around the growing plants.' If you do this, ensure that ash, lime and soot are around the plants, where it should reduce slug attacks, and not on their leaves, so as to avoid scorching, which greatly reduces the leaves' ability to photosynthesize.

How to catch a wireworm? Turn to Sam Beeton. 'If any bed or favourite plant suffers much from wireworm, a good trap may be made by placing small potatoes with a hole in them just under the surface of the ground, at different intervals. The wireworms will, in general, prefer this to any other food, and a daily examination will serve to entrap a great many of them.'

To rid carrots – and indeed all vegetables – of caterpillars, Columella in his *De Re Rustica* of *c.* AD 60 recommends shaking vegetables in the early morning, 'for if the caterpillars thus fall to the ground when they are still torpid from the night's cold, they no longer creep into the upper parts of the plant'. Or you could don camouflage and join Jane Loudon: 'A patent nostrum against caterpillar does not exist, but the careful cultivator will in good time look for patches of eggs and clusters of young caterpillars on the under sides of leaves, and will carefully nip off the leaves on which the colonies are seated, and make an end of them. This enemy cannot be taken in rank and file; he must be taken in detail, as in guerilla warfare.'

PARSNIPS

Thomas Hill outlines the health and curative properties of carrots and parsnips:

> Carots amend a cold reume, the paine of the stomack, stopping of urine, and chollick, a dry cough, the hard fetching of breath, the fluxe of the head, remove winde, heat the stomack, help the stopping of the liver, the vexing of the belly ... Parsneps and Carots removeth the venereall act, procureth Urine, and asswageth the Chollerick, sendeth downe the Termes in Women; it profiteth the Melanchollicke, encreaseth good blood, helpeth the straightnesse of making water, amendeth stitches of the sides or plurisies, the bite of venemous beast, it amendeth the eating of Ulcers, the wearing of this root is profitable.

Parsnips were the medieval staple root, appearing in Charlemagne's *Capitulare de villis* list, which in the ninth century instructed citizens of the Holy Roman Empire on what plants they should grow, and on the St Gall plan of *c.* AD 820 for a monastery garden; now carrots and potatoes have superseded them. They are slow growing – hence Hill's tip: 'Parsnep seeds may be sown in October, in the wane of the Moon; but if they prove not, sow more seeds in February following; and to make the roots the bigger and fairer in dry weather tread down the tops and leaves of them.' This suggestion may have been made because parsnip roots split if the weather gets too dry in summer, and if planted in autumn or late winter they will benefit from more rainfall than they would if planted later.

POTATOES

The *Solanaceae* or potato family has ninety genera and 2,600 species of shrubs, trees, lianes and herbs, with branched hairs and often prickles and alkaloids; it includes peppers and aubergines.

In 1600 the Frenchman Olivier de Serres writes of the potato, newly introduced to France: 'This plant, called cartoufle, bears fruits of the same name resembling truffles, and so called by some.'

Philip Miller lists potatoes under the name solanum, describing thirty-three varieties. He says: 'There are several other Species of this Plant, which are preserved in some curious Botanic Gardens for Variety; but those here mentioned being the most valuable Sorts I have observed in the English Gardens, I shall not enumerate the others ...' By 1905 there were many more varieties, William Robinson writing in *The Vegetable Garden*: 'Varieties of the Potato might be counted to the number of thousands ... The tubers, which are only underground branches swollen and filled with starchy matter, exhibit very great differences in shape and colour, according to varieties.'

Miller gives instructions for growing two types:

The red and white Potatoes ... were originally brought from Virginia into Europe, where they are at present so generally esteemed, as to be one of the most common esculent Roots now in Use. These Plants are propagated by planting the smallest Roots in Spring, which, in a good Soil, will multiply exceedingly; for I have many times seen ten, twelve, or more Roots produced from a single Off-set in one Year. The Soil on which these should be planted, ought to be rather moist than dry, and of a rich, soft, loose Texture; for if the Ground be too dry or binding, they will produce but very small Roots, and those but sparingly.

Note, though, the Reverend Henry Burgess's advice on soil in *The Amateur Gardener's Year-Book* (1854)– 'A Guide for those who cultivate their own gardens in the principles and practice of horticulture': '[ground for] Potatoes should not contain rich and exciting manures ...'

Miller continues: 'This Soil should be well dug or ploughed, and the small Roots laid in Trenches or Furrows six Inches deep, and about six Inches asunder in the Furrows: but the Furrows must be a Foot Distance from each other; for when they are too close, their Roots will not be large, which is what People usually covet.'

William Robinson more than doubles the planting distances in *The Vegetable Garden*: 'Potatoes are usually planted in April, in holes or pockets at a distance from one another of from 16in to 2ft, according to the vigour of growth of the variety.' Planting at these distances would increase the possibility of yield, but the crop would take up very much more space. He also says: 'Entire tubers of medium size are the best for planting. They should be covered, at the time of planting, with soil to the depth of 4 to 5 in, and the practice is to earth up as soon as the stems have grown to a height of 6 to 8 in; the ground being then also hoed for the second time.'

Miller, always an advocate of hoeing and keeping the ground clear of weeds, advises: 'In the Spring and Summer-months, the Weeds should be carefully hoed down between the Plants, until their Haulm is strong enough to bear them down, and prevent their Growth.'

Robinson's comment on earthing up is worth noting: 'The earthing-up is not absolutely necessary, but it has the advantage of causing the tubers to lie closer round the roots of the plant, so that they are more easily taken up.'

Potatoes can also successfully be produced in a large bucket – a method that lends itself to a competition for children to see who can produce the most potatoes in their bucket.

On harvesting, Miller says: 'and when their Haulm decays in Autumn, the roots may be taken up for Use; which may be done as they are wanted, till the Frost begins to set in.'

William Cobbett, the doyen of subsistence growing, loathed potatoes. In *Cottage Economy* (1823) he writes:

> I trust that we shall soon hear none of those savings, which the labourer makes by the use of potatoes. I hope we shall … leave Ireland to her lazy root … It is the root, also of slovenliness, filth, misery, and slavery; its cultivation has increased in

ABOVE *Marjolin Potato, aka Walnut-leaved Kidney, Sandringham Early Kidney, with smooth yellow skin and very yellow flesh, from William Robinson's* The Vegetable Garden.

England with the increase of the paupers: both, I thank God, are upon the decline. Englishmen seem to be upon the return to beer and bread, from water and potatoes; and, therefore, I shall now proceed to offer some observations to the Cottager, calculated to induce him to bake his own bread.

BRASSICAS

A medieval manuscript on cabbages advises:

> Take young Cabbages and set them in a ground that is greatly dunged, for in manner the ground where they shall be set cannot have too much dung, and let them be set every from other the space of the length of a yard; and always as they grow pluck off the lowest leaves, and so continue to the time that the leaves in the top begin to roll and to fold inwards, and then pluck no more of the leaves but let them grow, and they will grow round.

Since the ground around raspberries ought to be greatly 'dunged', too, it would be worth following the Reverend Henry Burgess's recommendation to 'never have two rows of Raspberries together, but to put them at distances sufficient to allow of the growth of cabbages, turnips, celery, etc., [in which case] every desirable end will be answered. In this case the canes need not be far apart individually, and a greater as well as a finer produce will be secured.'

When should we sow the poor man's medicine chest, as the French called the cabbage? Jane Loudon writes:

Cabbages for the autumn crop are sown in March, and one of the best kinds is the Vanack, as it is always in season, and as it sprouts freely from the stem after being cut; the sprouts indeed form such good heads that one plantation of this kind of cabbage might supply an amateur gardener with cabbages for a whole season. Among cabbages, the Battersea is very good for summer use; Aitkin's Matchless is also fine; the

Robinson illustrated Variegate Borecole, or Garnishing Kale, as a still life to emphasize that it is decorative for winter, both in the ground and on the table.

Rosette Colewort is the best to sow in May for autumn and early winter use; Green Curled Savoy and Early White Savoy are also good … The cabbages sown now should be transplanted in May or June; the seeds of cabbages for the main crops are sown in July and August. The seeds of the dwarf green Savoy and of the Asiatic cauliflower may also be sown in March.

Her husband John's decorative suggestion of sowing scarlet runners around the edges of a bed planted with cabbages fixes nitrogen in the soil.

PEAS

Peas were introduced by the Romans and mostly consumed dried. The delicate, sweet tastes of the first early peas became an expensive luxury. Richard Bradley wryly notes in *A General Treatise*: 'May 1723 … Forward Pease were sold this Month for Half a Guinea per Pottle-basket … Collyflowers of the right sort 5s … June 1723. About the Middle of the Month, most of the Crops of Pease and Beans about London were ripe, and came daily in such Quantities to the Markets, that their Price was reduced to about one shilling per Bushel.' A pottle is 2 quarts or half a gallon (2.25 litres) and a bushel is 8 gallons (9 litres). Like broad beans, peas are best eaten freshly picked.

On growing peas, Thomas Hill writes: 'Pease and Beanes for the Garden must have their seed changed every yeare, if not, the increase will be very smal, and grow lesse and lesse, for in three years, the great Rounseval and great Bean will be no bigger then the wild ones, do what you can to your ground, if you set or sow them which grew there before; and so likewise it is with Corn, if the seed be not changed.' This is curious advice because in fact as long as you save the largest, healthiest pods for seed your cropping should continue to be good.

Advice varies over whether peas and beans should be part of a four- or five-year crop rotation or grown in the same plot each year. On the question of when to sow, Hill advises: 'If you set Pease in February, set them an inch and a half deep, but if you set them in March or April, set them but an inch deep; but be sure you set them in the wane of the Moon, some six or seven days before the change, or else you will have a great Cod, and but smal Pease.' The disadvantage of sowing in February, however, would be that the seeds would be vulnerable to low temperatures (they are only moderately

hardy) and hungry mice. Try mulching during early development to conserve moisture, which will do as much good, if not more, as sowing by the phases of the moon. Hill continues: '... and let them be set from eight inches asunder And to have Pease long, and have them often, set them in several plots, some in February, some in March, and others in April: A quart of Pease will serve to set a good plot of ground; Pease and Beanes will prosper well being set under any Trees; and being sown in temperate wet weather, they will appear above ground in ten or twelve dayes, but being set in cold weather, it will be a moneth, or longer before they will appear.' Succession sowing is certainly a good system for domestic households, but it is surprising that Hill suggests growing under trees, as peas like an open sunny position, with a space between rows equal to their anticipated height.

SWEET CORN

Zea mays (*zea* from the Greek for cereal, *mays* the Mexican vernacular name) is known as maize, corn, sweet corn, Indian corn or Turkish corn. It originated in South America, and was cultivated by Aztecs, Mayas, Incas and other Indian tribes. Native American folklore recounts that a crow came from the south-west to the hunting grounds of the Narranganset Indians bearing a kernel of corn in one ear and in the other a bean. Both the corn and bean flourished and crows were never molested. For the Lenape Indians who lived in present-day Pennsylvania, corn was one of the three staple crops known as the three sisters, a stand of sweet corn with scarlet runners trained up them and a skirt of pumpkins – an ornamental and practical way of growing it if you have a rich, moisture-retentive soil.

In 1634 William Wood was impressed by the husbandry of the Indians in Connecticut in the cultivation of their sweet corn: '... [they] exceed our English husbandmen, keeping it as cleare with their Clamme-shell hoe as if it were a garden rather than a Cornfield, not suffering no choaking weede

ABOVE *The Gradus Pea, one of the earliest of the Victorian wrinkled peas, much prized for its great size and showy pods, illustrated in Robinson's* The Vegetable Garden.

to advance his audacious Head above their infant Corne, or an undermining Worme to spoil his Spurnes [roots].'

In Europe the first illustration of corn was in the frontispiece to Gerard's 1597 *Herball*, in which he describes it: 'Of Turkie Corn … it commeth to ripenesse when the summer falleth out to be faire and hot; as my selfe have seen by proof in myne owne garden. The Time It is sowen in these countries is March and Aprill, and the fruit is ripe in September … Turky wheat doth nourish far lesse than either wheat, rie, barly or otes.'

William Cobbett was as vehemently pro-sweet corn as he was anti-potatoes. Note the radical politician's rhetoric in his entry for it in *The English Gardener*.

CORN (Indian). – Infinite is the variety of the sorts of Indian corn, and great is the difference in the degrees of heat sufficient to bring the different sorts to perfection. Several of the sorts will seldom ripen well with the heat which they get in the state of New York, requiring that of Carolina or Virginia, at least. [This especially applies to corns with coloured kernels.] Other sorts will ripen perfectly well as far north as Boston; and there is a dwarf sort which will ripen equally well on land 500 miles to the north … Whether this be the same sort as that which I cultivate, I do not exactly know; but mine never fails to come to perfection in England, be the summer what it may. This is a very fine garden vegetable. The ear is stripped off the stalk just at the time when the grains are full of milk. The ears are then boiled for about twenty minutes: they are brought to table whole; each person takes an ear, rubs over it a little butter, and sprinkles it with a little salt, and bites the grains

1 *Frumentum Aſiaticum.*
Corne of Aſia.

Growing the golden sweet corn in England has come in and out of fashion, but North American and East European summers are best for multi-coloured cobs.

from the stalk to which they are attached, and which in America is called the cob. In the Indian corn countries, every creature likes Indian corn better than any other vegetable, not excepting even the fine fruits of those countries. When dead ripe, the grains are hard as any grain can be; and upon this grain, without any grinding, horses are fed, oxen are fatted, hogs are fatted and poultry made perfectly fat by eating the grain whole tossed down to them in the yard. The finest turkeys in the whole world are fatted in this way, without the least possible trouble. Nothing can be easier to raise. The corn is planted along little drills about three or four feet apart, the grains at four inches apart in the drill … during the first fortnight in May. When it is out of the ground about two inches, the ground should be nicely moved all over, and particularly near to the plants. [This is the time to sow your runner beans and pumpkins if you want the three sisters.] When the plants attain to the height of a foot, the ground should be dug between them, and a little earth should be put up about the stems. When the plants attain the height of a foot and a half or two feet, another digging should take place, and the stems of the plants should be earthed up to another four or five inches: after this you have nothing to do but keep the ground clear from weeds … about three rows across one of the plats in the garden would be sufficient for any family.

Matthew Arnold evokes the beauty of ripe corn in 'The Dream':

> Back'd by the pines, a plank built cottage stood
> Bright in the sun; the climbing gourd plant's leaves
> Muffled its walls, and on the stone strewn roof
> Lay the warm golden gourds of golden within;
> Under the eaves, pear'd rows of Indian corn.

In a tract Cobbett wrote in 1847 – 'a case for the Time … showing the practicability and necessity of cultivating Maize' – he itemized maize's many uses: the husks for stuffing mattresses, to make door mats and in brown paper production; pitch of cob as an excellent fuel; the stalks to light fires and heat the bread oven all winter; and as fodder for pigs to make good bacon – and they can be smoked by the burning stalks.

Leaves and herbs

What diversities soever there be in herbs, all are shuffled up together under the name of a sallade.

Michel de Montaigne (1533–92)

HERBES AND ROOTES FOR SALLETS AND SAUCE

Alexanders, at all times.

Artichoks.

Blessed thistle, or Carduus benedictus

Cucumbers in April & May

Cresies, sowe with Lettice in the spring

Endive.

Mustard seede, sowe in the spring and Mihelmas

Musk million, in April and May

Mints.

Purslane.

Radish, & after remove them

Rampions.

Rokat, in April.

Sage.

Sorell.

Spinage, for the sommer.

Sea holie.

Sperage, let growe two yeares, and then remove.

Skirrets, set these plants in March.

Suckerie.

Tarragon, set in slippes in March

Violets of all coulors.

Thomas Tusser, *Five Hundred Points of Good Husbandry* (1573)

The word salad stems from the Italian *zelada,* a dish devised for festivities in fifteenth-century Milan, consisting of a salty ragout flavoured with preserves, mustard and lemon, and decorated with marzipan. While Tusser's list certainly includes several plants that would need cooking with a pinch of salt before being added warm or cold to a salad, the following medieval list of salad plants (cited by Alicia Amherst in *A History of Gardening in England*) reads more like a chaplet or garland: 'Herbes for a Salade Buddus of Stanmarche, Vyolette flourez, Percely, Redmynte, Syves, Cresse of Boleyn, Purselan, Ramsons, Calamynte, Prime rose buddus, Dayses, Rapounses, Daundelyon, Rokette, Red nettell, Borage flourez, Croppus of Red Fenell, Selbestryn, Chkynwede.' All these plants, young, tender and tangy in April and May, would have provided a vitamin boost after a limited winter diet.

John Evelyn's definition of salads in *Acetaria, A Discourse on Sallets* (published in 1699), which he wrote when he was nearly eighty, accords more with our modern idea of them:

> Sallets in general consist of certain Esculent plants and Herbs, improved by culture, industry and art of the gardener: or as others say, they are a composition of Edule Plants and Roots of several kinds, to be eaten raw or green, blanched or candied; simple and per se, or

Has today's gardener lost the flair for headgear? This gardener was snapped c. 1925 against a 'Mary, Mary quite contrary' backdrop but her barrow and superlative chard speak volumes of her parentage.

intermingled with others according to the season ... we are by Sallet
to understand a particular composition of certain Crude and fresh
Herbs, such as usually are, or may safely be eaten with some acetous
juice, oyl, salt, etc to give them a grateful gust and vehicle.

An example of a root that makes a good salad vegetable is the beetroot,
praised by Gerard in his 1597 *Herball*, in which he says: 'Being eaten when
it is boyled, it nourisheth little or nothing, and is not so wholesome as
Lettuce [but] The great and beautifull Beet ... may be used in Winter for a
sallad herb, ... is not only pleasant to the taste, but also delightfull to the eie.
The greater red Beet or Roman beet, boyled and eaten with oyle, vinegre
and pepper, is a most excellent and delicat salad.'

ABOVE *Another stereoscope shot, making viewers feel that they are amongst the dangling cucumbers
which effectively shade the fern collection.*

Hill puts readers of *The Gardener's Labyrinth* (1577) to work on salad plants in May: 'And the same Garden-plot or quarters of the Garden, which the Gardener would in the harvest time have covered with the Sallet, pot hearbs and roots, ought to be turned up in the beginning of the summer, or in the moneth of May, that the clods of earth ... be so dissolved.'

LETTUCE

'The lettuce is to me a most interesting study. Lettuce is like conversation; it must be fresh and crisp, so sparkling that you scarcely notice the bitter of it. Lettuce, like most talkers, is, however, apt to run rapidly to seed. Blessed is that sort which comes to a head, and so remains, like a few people I know; growing more solid and satisfactory and tender at the same time, and whiter at the centre and crisp in their maturity.' With C.D. Warner's words from *My Summer in a Garden* (1918) lettuce takes on a new dimension. All lettuce – and today we grow a wide variety of types, for which we have to thank the writer and nurserywoman Joy Larkcom who introduced many salad leaves to modern gardeners – is a thousand times crisper and better when harvested straight from the garden.

For a description of the active ingredients of lettuce, we can turn to Maude Grieve's *A Modern Herbal* (1931): 'The name lactuca is derived from the classical Latin name for the milky juice, virosa, or poisonous ... The whole plant is rich in a milky juice that flows freely from any wound. This has a bitter taste and a narcotic odour ... All lettuces possess some of this narcotic juice.' Which explains why lettuce seedlings had a soporific effect on Beatrix Potter's Flopsy Bunnies.

In four pages of *The Culture of Vegetables and Flowers* (1913) devoted to growing solid, satisfactory and tender lettuces Suttons & Sons elaborate on the qualities of lettuce:

THE LETTUCE is the king of salads, and as a cooked vegetable it has its value; but as it does not compete with the Pea, the Asparagus, or the Cauliflower, we need not make comparisons ... Scientific advisers on diet and health esteem the Lettuce highly for its anti-scorbutic properties, and especially for its wholesomeness as a corrective. It supplies the blood with vegetable juices that are needful to accompany flesh foods when cooked vegetables are unattainable.

The numerous varieties may, for practical purposes, be grouped in two classes – Cabbage and Cos Lettuces … the first group being invaluable for mixed salads at all seasons, but more especially in winter and early spring; the second group is most serviceable in the summer season, and is adapted for a simple kind of salad, the leaves being more crisp and juicy … In the selection of sorts, leading types should be kept in view. Some of the varieties which have been introduced have no claim to a place in a good list, because of their coarseness … The best types are tender and delicately flavoured, representing centuries of cultivation …

On how to grow lettuces, Gerard refers to classical sources. 'Palladius saith …[it should be sown in] a mannured, fat, moist, and dunged ground: it must be sowen in faire weather in places where there is plenty of water, as Columella saith, and prospereth best if it be sowen very thin.'

Suttons & Sons say:

The Lettuce requires a light, rich soil, but almost any kind of soil may be so prepared as to ensure a fair supply … and fat stable manure should be liberally used. The best way to prepare ground for the summer crop is to select a piece that has been trenched, and go over it again, laying in a good body of rough green manure, one spade deep, so that the plant will be put on unmanured ground, but will reach the manure at the very period when it is needed, by which time contact with the earth will have rendered it sweet and mellow. By this mode of procedure the finest growth is secured, and the plants stand well without bolting as they are saved from the distress consequent on continued dry weather.

According to Beeton's *Shilling Gardener* of the 1860s: 'A north border is a good situation in which to plant during the summer months, as the plants are less exposed to the sun, grow stronger, are more succulent and crisp, and are longer before they run to seed.' Equally try growing lettuce around trees or shrubs or as decorative temporary edgings for a potager. Lettuce also makes an excellent catch crop between other vegetables and herbs.

For 'successive sowings (under glass) made in February and March' Suttons & Sons advise: 'In planting out, it is important to have the seedlings well hardened, for they are naturally susceptible to wind and sunshine, and if suddenly exposed to either will be likely to perish.'

All leaf crops are susceptible to slugs and snails and *The Times* of 16 March 1907 is not hopeful about the prospects of getting rid of them:

> Slugs and snails are perhaps the worst pests of a heavy soil, and there is no means of extirpating them. They can only be dealt with in detail by killing all that are encountered and by surrounding the plants for which they have particular fancy with soot or ashes. Not only is the voracity of slugs, though vegetarian, comparable with that of sharks and crocodiles when the difference of size is considered, but they have also a horrible epicurism of taste which will not be satisfied by an innocent meal off the leaves of vigorous and full-grown plants. They make for whatever is young and tender, and are happy only when they can kill where they dine. Where they abound, therefore, seedlings should not be exposed to them until they have outgrown their first delicacy.

However, if today's popular deterrents of beer traps, frogs and hedgehogs fail, you might consider using your lettuce crop as a trap, as advised by Suttons & Sons: 'Again, when first planted out their delicate leaves will attract all the slugs and snails in the garden, and the discreet way of acting is to regard a plantation of Lettuce as an extensive vermin trap, and thus, knowing where the marauders are, to be ready to catch and kill, or to destroy them by sprinklings of lime, salt, or soot, in all cases being careful to keep these agents at a reasonable distance from the plants.'

SPINACH

Popeye consumed his spinach cooked and research at the Department of Pharmacy at Angers University suggests that if you eat spinach cooked the nutritional gain is greater because you can eat a far greater quantity of it than raw spinach. Evelyn preferred it cooked: 'Spinach, Spinachia: of old not us'd in Sallets, and the oftener kept out the better; I speak of the crude: But being boil'd to a Pult, and without other water than its own moisture, is a most excellent Condiment with Butter, Vinegar, or Limon, for almost all sorts of boil'd Flesh, and may accompany a Sick Man's Diet. 'Tis Laxative and Emollient, and therefore profitable for the Aged, and (tho' by original a Spaniard) may be had at almost any Season, and in all places.'

Spinach featured in Maude Grieve's herbal, in which she explains:

Spinach should be grown on good ground, well worked and well manured, and for the summer crops abundant water will be necessary.

To afford a succession of Summer Spinach, the seeds should be sown about the middle of February and again in March. After this period, small quantities should be sown once a fortnight, as Summer Spinach lasts a very short time. The seeds are generally sown in shallow drills, between the lines of peas. If occupying the whole of a plot, the rows should be 1 foot apart.

The Round-seeded is the best kind for summer use.

The Prickly-seeded and the Flanders kinds are the best for winter and should be thinned out early in the autumn to about 2 inches apart, and later on to 6 inches. The Lettuce-leaved, is a good succulent winter variety but not quite so hardy.

Philip Miller, who was aware of maximising space, advises readers of *The Gardener's Dictionary* (1731) with a small plot to sow spinach 'upon an open Spot of Ground by themselves, or else mixed with Radish-seed, as is the common Practice of the Gardeners near London, who always endeavour to have as many Crops from their Land in a Season as possible'.

PARSLEY

There is an old superstition against transplanting parsley plants and they certainly fare better if sown and thinned in the same place. John Gardener wrote about parsley in *The Feate of Gardening* (c. 1440), from which you could harvest some good advice, if you can work your way around the language:

> Percell kynde ys for to be
> To be sow yn the monthe of mars so mote y the
> He will grow long and thykke
> And euer as he growyth thu schalt hym kytte
> Thu may hym kytte by reson'
> Thryes yn one seson'
> Wurtys to make and sewes also.
> Let him never to hye go
> To lete hym grow to hye hit is grete foly.

If you enjoy the look of curled parsley (*Petroselenium crispum*) you could try Gerard's experiment: 'If you will have the leaves of the parcelye grow crisped, then before the sowing of them stuffe a tennis ball with the seedes and beat the same well against the ground whereby the seedes maybe of little bruised or when the parcelye is well come up go over the bed with a waighty roller whereby it may so presse the leaves down or else tread the same downe under thy feet.'

The doyenne of herbal expertise Maude Grieve advises:

For a continuous supply, three sowings should be made: as early in February as the weather permits, in April or early in May and in July and early August – the last being for the winter supply, in a sheltered position, with a southern exposure. Sow in February for the summer crop and for drying purposes. Seed sown then, however, takes several weeks to germinate, often as much as a full month. The principal sowing is generally done in April; it then germinates more quickly and provides useful material for cutting throughout the summer. A mid-August sowing will furnish good plants for placing in the cold frames for winter use. An even broadcast sowing is preferable, if the ground is in the condition to be trodden, which appears to fix the seed in its place, and after raking leaves a firm even surface ...

Beeton's *New Dictionary of Every-Day Gardening* gives very specific instructions on how to create a parsley bed: '... remove the soil to the depth of six or eight inches, and fill in the bottom with the same depth of stones, brick-rubbish, and similar loose material. Over this prepare the bed of light rich soil, which will thus be raised considerably above the level of the ground, the bed being raked smooth and level. Towards the end of May, sow some seed of the most curly variety ...' This advice recalls the fact that parsley seeds have the maddening habit of germinating very successfully on rubble piles which sadly cannot sustain them.

Mrs Grieve continues: 'When the seedlings are well out of the ground, about an inch high, adequate thinning is imperative ... and about 8 inches from plant to plant must be allowed: a well-grown plant will cover nearly a square foot of ground. If the growth becomes coarse in the summer, cut off all the leaves and water well. This will induce a new growth of fine leaves, and may always be done when the plants have grown to a good size, as it encourages a stocky growth.' This last point also applies to lovage and chives, which can be thus stimulated to provide fresh leaves to late autumn – and equally to many herbaceous perennials in flower borders.

She also advises: 'Soon after the old or last year's plants begin to grow again in the spring, they run to flower, but if the flower stems are promptly removed, and the plants top dressed and watered, they will remain productive for some time longer. Renew the beds every two years, as the plant dies down at the end of the second season.'

Folklore about parsley abounds. As it is notoriously fickle about germinating, the tradition of sowing it on Good Friday may relate to a belief that germination would be helped by the association with the Resurrection. Parsley was an essential green herb; hence the saying 'Where the parsley stays green all year round, the wife wears the trousers' indicated that the woman was in control of the health and welfare of her household.

FINES HERBES

Parsley is one of the *fines herbes*, the others being chives, French tarragon and chervil. To grow chervil, which has a delicate aniseed taste, and can

" A rich array of fragrant tasteful herbs
Did bounteous Nature give: sweet balm to lull
The fever-quickened pulse; basil, plant royal;
And borage, dressing meat for cooling cup."
ANON.

ABIA'NA (*nat. ord.* Irida'cœœ). Dwarf, free-flowering, half-hardy Cape bulbs of great beauty, that do well in a sandy, peaty soil, and sheltered sunny situation out of doors, but best suited for cold greenhouse. If planted in open borders the bulbs should be taken up in autumn. When the bulbs are sending up leaves and flowers they should be kept well watered. There are many varieties, bearing blue, purple, blue and white, dark red, red and white, red and yellow, and yellow blossoms. The best known perhaps is *Babiana villosa*, with flowers of a delicate violet, blooming in August.

Balm (*nat. ord.* Labia'tæ).
A sweet-scented hardy herbaceous pe-

rennial(*Melissa officinalis*) with ornamental foliage, succeeding in any common garden soil. Propagated by divisions of the roots in March or October. In former times,

BALM.

owing to the lemon-like flavour of the leaves, it was much used in making a cooling drink, known as balm tea.

B is for beauty and bounty and, here, Beeton's Brussel sprouts, belladonna lily, basil, beans, broccoli and browallia.

provide pickings for almost ten months of the year, simply follow the advice of Suttons & Sons: 'To secure a regular supply of leaves small successional sowings are necessary from spring to autumn ... For winter use, sow in boxes kept in a warm temperature.' It also usefully seeds itself.

French tarragon does not set from seed (only the thuggish, tasteless Russian tarragon does). Eleanour Sinclair Rohde, who gardened at at Cranham Lodge, Reigate in Surrey and whose early twentieth-century writings inspired me to grow herbs, describes it in *Herbs and Herb Gardening* (1936) in flavoursome prose that is redolent of the herb itself: 'French Tarragon is the one esteemed as a salad herb. This Tarragon is a native of Central Asia and it was not known in Europe till early Tudor times ... as Gerard observed three hundred years ago 'the flowers never perfectly open' ... It is one of the most valuable kitchen herbs and too seldom grown nowadays ... John Evelyn, commends Tarragon as being 'highly cordial and friendly to the head, heart, and liver' ... The Tarragons like a sandy soil, shelter from cold winds, and though they like a warm spot, they do not object to part shade. They are increased by division in April.' French tarragon is an ideal subject for a large terracotta pot provided it is kept dry and sheltered during the winter.

Revel in Henry Lyte's description of chives in *A Niewe Herball of Historie of Plantes* (1578): 'Cyves or Rushe Onyons ... have little smal, holowe, and slender piped blades, lyke to smale Rushes', and written twenty years later, Gerard's:

Cives bring forth many leaves about a hand-full high, long slender,

round, like to little rushes; amongst which grow up small and tender stalkes, sending forth certain crops with floures like those of the Onion but much lesser. They have many little bulbes or headed roots fastened together; out of which grow downe in the earth a great number of little strings, and it hath both the taste of Onion and Leeke, as it were participating of both.

An engraving from Thornton's Family Herbal *of lemon balm, a potent sharpener of wits and humour. Control it in the garden by eating it regularly.*

Gerard also says: 'Cives are set in gardens, they floureth long, and continue many yeares, they suffer the cold of winter. They are cut and poled often, as is the unset Leeke.' That is, if cut they come again.

J.C. Loudon says: 'No cottage garden ought to be without the Chive; it forms one of the most wholesome herbs for chopping up and mixing among the food for young chickens, ducks, and turkeys - making them thrive wonderfully, and preventing that pest the gripes.' Strangely he makes no mention of chopping them up for the household.

BASIL

Basil tingles the spine and the taste buds. 'Curse when you sow basil' is an excellent tip. Choose a time when you are hot and bothered. Basil germinates with the greatest of ease but it often fails to grow on. It likes a rich soil that drains very quickly, so never water a failing basil seedling. The soil should contain blood and bonemeal, because 'basil thrives on dead men's entrails'. Tusser rightly recommends sowing it in a terracotta pot, starting in May:

> Fine bazell sowe, in a pot to growe
> Fine seedes sowe now, before ye sawe how.
> Fine bazell desireth it may be hir lot,
> to growe as the gilloflower, trim in a pot,
> That ladies and gentils, for whom she doth serve,
> may helpe hir as needeth, poore life to preserve.

Nicholas Culpeper was an astrologer-physician, with a practice based in Spitalfields in London, who was reviled for translating the *Pharmacopoea* to make it accessible to common man in 1652. The translation, *The English Physitian* became his *Herbal*, which weaves together medicine, astrology and practical advice, and in which he writes of basil:

Galen and Dioscorides hold it is not fitting to be taken inwardly and Chrysippus rails at it. Pliny and the Arabians defend it. Something is the matter, this herb and rue will not grow together, no, nor near one another, and we know rue is as great an enemy to poison as any that grows.

Being applied to the place bitten by venomous beasts or stung by a wasp or hornet, it speedily draws the poison to it. Every like draws its like. Mizaldus affirms, that being laid to rot in horse-dung, it will breed venomous beasts. Hilarius, a French physician, affirms upon his own knowledge, that an acquaintance of his, by common smelling to it, had a scorpion breed in his brain.

John Evelyn includes basil in his *Acetaria*, writing of it: 'Basil, Ocimum (as Baulm) imparts a grateful Flavour, if not too strong, somewhat offensive to the Eyes; and therefore the tender Tops to be very sparingly us'd in our Sallets.'

Basil is a perennial. Suttons & Sons advise: 'Many gardeners lift plants in September, pot them [and bring them indoors], and so maintain a supply of fresh green leaves until winter is far advanced.' You can then replant the next year but I have found the winter pickings very small. Many basil plants bought in supermarkets transfer well into the ground in summer.

Fruiting vegetables

AUBERGINES

The aubergine (*Solanum melongena*) is in the potato family. It is also known as brinjal, eggplant or garden egg, and was formerly referred to as a madde apple. It probably originated in India with secondary centres of diversity in

A photograph of c. 1915, proudly captioned 'Ye pergola – a new kitchen garden on right: pond garden on left – can you see Sirje grubbing here, putting seeds and things'.

South East Asia, particularly China, and was introduced into Europe in the thirteenth century.

Three hundred years after its introduction it was still viewed with suspicion. Gerard's description in his 1597 *Herball*, as always, paints a vivid portrait:

Of Madde Apples

The Description. Raging Apples hath a round stalke of two foot high, divided into sundry branches, set with broad leaves somewhat indented about the edges, not unlike the leaves of white Henbane, of a darke browne greene colour, somewhat rough. Among the which come the floures of a white colour, and sometimes changing into purple, made of six pairs wide open like a star, with certain yellow chives or thrums in the middle: which being past the fruit comes in place, set in a cornered cup or huske after the manner of great Nightshade, great and somewhat long, of the bignesse of a Swans Egge, and sometimes much greater, of a white colour, sometimes yellow, and often brown, wherein is contained small flat seed of a yellow colour. The root is thick, with many threds fastned thereto.

The Place. This Plant growes in Egypt almost every where in sandy fields even of it selfe, bringing forth fruit of the bignesse of a great Cucumber ... We had the same in our London gardens, where it hath borne floures; ... it came to beare fruit of the bignes of a goose egg one extraordinarie temperate yeare, as I did see in the garden of a worshipfull merchant Mr. Harvy in Limestreet; but never to the full ripenesse.

The Use, and Danger. The people of Toledo eat them with great devotion ... But I rather wish English men to content themselves with the meat and sauce of our owne country, than with fruit and sauce eaten with such perill; for doubtlesse these Apples have a mischievous qualitie, the use whereof is utterly to be foresaken. ... it is therefore better to esteem this plant and have it in the garden for your pleasure and the rarenesse therof, than for any vertue or good qualities yet knowne.

There may be a grain of truth in the idea of the aubergine having a 'mischievous quality'. A delicious Turkish aubergine recipe is called *imam bayaldi*, meaning 'the priest has fainted' – that is, that he swooned with gastronomical joy at the fragrant odour.

Six hundred years after its introduction, Beeton is cautious about the aubergine, mentioning only its ornamental use in his *New Dictionary of Every-Day Gardening*: 'Egg-plant. A very singular and ornamental class of fruit-bearing half-hardy annuals, especially adapted for conservatory or drawing-room decoration: they thrive best in very rich light soil.' The leaves are attractively pupescent (covered with short, fine, soft hairs) and the ragged purple flowers are interesting.

William Robinson's translation of Vilmorin-Andrieux's *The Vegetable Garden* explains how to grow the aubergine: 'In the climate of Paris the Egg-plant can seldom be grown without the aid of artificial heat. The seed is usually sown on a hot-bed in February or March, and the seedlings are pricked out into another hot-bed six weeks or two months later. Early varieties raised in hot-beds may also be planted out in the open air about the end of May, when the ground has become well warmed. The plants require a warm and sheltered position, and plentiful waterings. In order to obtain handsome, well-grown fruit, a certain number only should be allowed to remain on each plant, proportioned to its strength.' Unless you have an exceptionally warm and sheltered garden, aubergines only fruit successfully under glass or plastic. They are heavy feeders, so use good growbags or large pots rather than small pots, and you will need to select just a few fruits per bush as Robinson says.

He goes on: 'It is a good plan also to pinch the extremities of the branches towards the end of the summer. In England we have never seen this plant well grown even under glass. In the Eastern States of North America we were surprised at the fine health it attained in the fields, and the great size of the fruit – as large as well-grown Melons.'

He describes two kinds:

New York Purple Eggplant … Fruit very large, of a very short Pear shape, and slightly flattened at both ends; it is paler in colour than that of the Round Purple Egg-plant, but is larger and fuller and entirely devoid of ribs or longitudinal furrows … This variety is distinguished from those already enumerated by its lower stature, its

ABOVE *Robinson illustrated the white aubergine, noting that is not fit to eat but useful for ornamenting baskets of mixed fruits at dessert.*

more compact and thick-set habit, and especially by the quality of the flesh, which almost entirely fills the interior of the fruit, leaving but very little space for the seeds. A plant seldom carries more than two fruit.

White Egg-Plant A rather low-growing, branching plant … fruit white, exactly resembling a hen's egg, but turning yellow when ripe … its chief use is for ornament. The fruit is (probably erroneously) considered by some to be unwholesome … The fruit is not eaten, but may be used as ornaments in baskets of mixed fruits at dessert, etc.

The New York purple aubergine is available today and there is a modern white variety, 'Palomo', that is certainly worth eating.

TOMATOES

Another member of the *Solanaceae* family, in the genus *Lycopersicon* (from the Greek *lykos* meaning wolf and *persikon* meaning peach), the tomato was traditionally known as the love-apple. South American Indians explained to the Moriscos, the first Andalusian colonists, that this fruit *tomatl* made good sauces if flavoured with *ahi* (chilli pepper). The Italians chose to call them *pomodoro* and the Provencals *pommes d'amour*.

As with the other solanums – potatoes and aubergines – Gerard was the first to describe them, which he does with his usual superb eye for detail:

Of Apples of Love
The Apple of Love bringeth forth very long round stalkes or branches, fat and full of juice, trailing upon the ground, not able to sustain himselfe upright by reason of the tendernesse of the stalkes, and also the great weight of the leaves and fruit wherewith it is surcharged. The leaves are great, and deeply cut or jagged about the edges, not unlike to the leaves of Agrimonie, but greater, and of a whiter greene colour: Amongst which come forth yellow floures growing upon short stems or footstalkes, clustering together in bunches: which being fallen there doe come in place fair and goodly apples, chamfered, uneven, and bunched out in many places; of a bright shining red colour, and the bignesses of a goose egge or a large pippin. The pulpe or meat is very full of moisture, soft, reddish, and of the substance of a wheat plumme. The seed is small, flat and rough:

the root small and threddy: the whole plant is of a ranke and stinking savour ... There happened unto my hands another sort, ... the fruit hereof was yellow.

The Place   Apples of Love grow in Spain, Italie, and such hot Countries, from whence my selfe have received seeds for my garden, where they doe increase and prosper.

The Time   It is sowne in the beginning of Aprill in a bed of hot horse-dung, after the manner of muske Melons and such like cold fruits.

By the mid eighteenth century Miller was able to list eight varieties in his *Gardener's Dictionary* including red, yellow, white and cherry varieties. Less than a hundred years later Cobbett includes the tomato as a plant for larger gardens. He describes it: 'Tomatum   This plant comes from countries bordering on the Mediterranean. Of sorts there are the red, the yellow, and the white. The fruit is used for various purposes, and is sold at a pretty high price.' Prosperous Edwardian gardeners grew and consumed them, and in *Lark Rise to Candleford* the young Laura bought a 'love-apple'.

In a section on glass Thompson's *Gardener's Assistant* (1880) says:

The Tomato, or Love Apple ... is now very extensively cultivated for its fruit, which forms the principal ingredient of various sauces, but is more valued as a salad, immense quantities being eaten in an uncooked state, with condiments varying with the tastes of those who eat them ... Extensive trials of Tomatoes are held periodically in the Royal Horticultural Gardens at Chiswick, and the reports published in the Journal of the Society have been of considerable assistance in the preparation of this chapter. Upwards of one hundred varieties of Tomatoes, more or less distinct, are now available for cultivation ...

All writers acknowledge that the tomato, which was domesticated in Mexico and Central America, needs a warm start. If you do not have a heated greenhouse or soil-warming cables, a traditional hotbed is worth experimenting with. Miller writes: 'Lycopersicon, Love-apple ... These Plants are propagated by sowing their Seeds on a moderate Hot-bed in March; and when come up, they should be transplanted into another moderate Hot-bed, at about three Inches Distance from each other, observing to shade them until they have taken Root; after which they must have frequent Waterings, and a large Share of fresh Air; for if they are too much drawn while young, they seldom do well afterwards.' Current thinking is that you should wait for the first flowers to set before moving them on to their final situation.

Cobbett echoes: 'The plants must be raised in a gentle hot-bed pretty early in April, or late in March, put into small pots when they are two inches high, and turned out into the natural ground about the first week in June; but even then they must be put on the south side of a wall, or in some other warm and sheltered situation.'

Thompson, writing when labour, rather than labour saving, was the watchword, says:

Late in March, or the first week in April, is soon enough to sow the seed, and the preference should be given to moderately strong-growing, free-setting, early-maturing varieties – notably Champion, Frogmore Selected, Early Ruby, Golden Nugget, Holmes' Supreme, Comet, and Veitch's Glory, all of which are heavy croppers [all, sadly,

from Weeds, and in very dry Weather repeat watering them as often as they shall want it ; and when they have obtained sufficient Strength to remove, they may be transplanted either into Pots or Borders, where they are to remain. By this Method you may greatly increase these Plants, which will supply the Defect of Seeds.

LYCOPERSICON, Love-apple.

The *Characters* are ;

It hath a Flower consisting of one Leaf, which expands in a circular Order, as doth that of the Nightshade ; the Style afterwards becomes a roundish soft fleshy Fruit, wherein is divided into several Cells, wherein are contained many flat Seeds.

The *Species* are ;

1. LYCOPERSICON *Galeni.* Ang. Yellow Love-apple.

2. LYCOPERSICON *Galeni, fructu rubro. Boerh. Ind.* Love-apple with a red Fruit.

3. LYCOPERSICON *fructu cerasi rubro. Tourn.* Love-apple with a red cherry-shaped Fruit.

4. LYCOPERSICON *fructu cerasi luteo. Tourn.* Love-apple with a yellow cherry-shaped Fruit.

5. LYCOPERSICON *fructu striato duro. Tourn.* Love-apple with an hard channelled Fruit.

6. LYCOPERSICON *fructu rubro non striato. Inst. R. H.* Love-apple with a smooth red Fruit.

7. LYCOPERSICON *fructu albo. Inst. R. H.* Love-apple with a white Fruit.

8. LYCOPERSICON *Americanum arborescens, amplissimis foliis angulatis. Plum. Cat. American* tree-like Love-apple, with large angular Leaves.

These Plants are propagated by sowing their Seeds on a moderate Hot-bed in *March* ; and when come

up, they should be transplanted into another moderate Hot-bed, at about three Inches Distance from each other, observing to shade them until they have taken Root ; after which they must have frequent Waterings, and a large Share of fresh Air ; for if they are too much drawn while young, they seldom do well afterwards.

In *May* these Plants should be transplanted, either into Pots filled with rich light Earth, or into the Borders of the Flower-garden, observing to water and shade them until they have taken Root ; and as the Branches are extended, they should be supported with Sticks ; otherwise, when the Fruit begins to grow, it will press them down, and break them.

Those Plants which are placed in Pots, should be often watered, otherwise they will come to little ; for they are very droughty Plants : but when they are planted in a rich moist Soil, they will grow to a prodigious Size, and produce large Quantities of Fruit ; which in Autumn, when they are ripe, make an odd Figure ; but the Plants emit so strong an Effluvium, as renders them unfit to stand near an Habitation, or any Place that is much frequented ; for upon their being brushed by the Cloaths, they send forth a very strong disagreeable Scent.

The *Italians* and *Spaniards* eat these Apples, as we do Cucumbers, with Pepper, Oil, and Salt ; and some eat them stewed in Sawces, &c. but, considering their great Moisture and Coldness, the Nourishment they afford must be bad. The first of these Plants is the Sort directed for medicinal Use, by the College in their Dispensatory.

The sixth and seventh Sorts are annual Plants, which perish soon after

they have perfected their Fruit. These must be sown in the Spring on a moderate Hot-bed to bring them forward, and afterward treated in the same manner as these Sorts which are mentioned before.

The eighth Sort will rise to the Height of six or eight Feet, and become woody. This Sort is propagated by Seeds, which should be sown on an Hot-bed in the Spring ; and when the Plants are come up about two Inches high, they must be transplanted into a moderate Hot-bed, observing to water and shade them until they have taken new Root ; after which time they should have a large Share of free Air in warm Weather, to prevent their drawing up weak. When the Plants have obtained a good Share of Strength, they should be carefully taken up with the Earth to their Roots, and planted into Pots filled with light rich Earth, and placed in a shady Situation until they have taken Root ; when they may be removed into a warm Situation, where they may remain abroad in the open Air, until the Middle or End of *September,* when they must be removed into the Conservatory, and placed where they may have a moderate Share of Warmth in cold Weather ; by which Method the Plants may be preserved through the Winter, and the following Summer they will produce Fruit.

LYCOPUS, Water Horehound.

This Plant grows in great Plenty on moist Soils by the Sides of Ditches in most Parts of *England* ; but is never cultivated in Gardens, so that it would be needless to say any thing more of it in this Place.

LYSIMACHIA, Loose-strife.

The *Characters* are ;

The Leaves, which are intire and

oblong, are produced sometimes by Pairs, or three or four at each Joint of the Stalk ; the Flower consists of one Leaf, which expands in a circular Order, and is cut into several Segments at the Top ; the Fruit is globular, and opens at the Top, inclosing many Seeds fixed to the Placenta.

The *Species* are ;

1. LYSIMACHIA *lutea major, quæ Dioscoridis. C. B. P.* Common yellow Loose-strife or Willow-herb.

2. LYSIMACHIA *lutea major, quæ Dioscoridis, foliis quaternis. C. B. P.* Greater yellow Loose-strife or Willow-herb, with four Leaves at each Joint.

3. LYSIMACHIA *bifolia, flore luteo globoso. C. B. P.* Loose-strife with two Leaves growing at each Joint, and yellow Flowers growing in round Heads.

4. LYSIMACHIA *orientalis angustifolia, flore purpureo. T. Cor.* Narrow-leaved Eastern Loose-strife, with a purple Flower.

5. LYSIMACHIA *Hispanica spicata, flore purpureo. Josf. Spanish* Loose-strife, with purple Flowers growing in Spikes.

The first of these Plants is pretty common by Ditch-sides in many Parts of *England,* and is seldom cultivated in Gardens ; tho' it is not a very despicable Plant ; for it produces large Spikes of fine yellow Flowers in *July,* for which Reason it may be admitted into a cold wet Part of the Garden, where few others will thrive ; whereby many a Spot of Ground may be rendered agreeable, which often produces little, but gross Weeds. This Plant may be taken up in the Spring, from the native Places of its Growth, and transplanted where you intend it should grow ; and it will soon increase by its creeping Roots, to what

Philip Miller describes eight colours and shapes of Lycopersicon or love-apple and how to eat them. He makes no mention of the name tomato.

no longer available].

The seeds should be sown thinly in well-drained 6 inch pots, or in pans and boxes, using light sandy soil, and placed on or plunged in a mild hot-bed, or, failing this, on a bed or staging in a forcing house or frame of any kind. If the soil is kept uniformly moist [not damp] the seedlings will appear in a week to ten days. Before they become leggy, raise them up to the light in the same house, pit, or frame, and thin out if necessary.

When they have formed two leaves above the cotyledons, either plant them singly in the centre of 3 inch or 4 inch pots, or in pairs against the sides of 6 inch pots. Light loamy soil, previously warmed by means of hot bricks plunged in the heap, should be used [today we can warm compost by placing black plastic over it in advance], and the plants ought to be buried up to their seed-leaves. If they can be given the benefit of bottom-heat and a little shade they will quickly recover from the check given, but if the house or pit can be kept at from 60° to 70°, bottom heat may be dispensed with. Water carefully at first, especially where the larger pots are used, but when they are growing strongly much more water will be needed, and the plants must also be raised well up to the light to prevent them from becoming leggy. When small pots are used the plants should be shifted again into 6 inch pots, otherwise they quickly become root-bound and starved. On the whole it is better to place the seedlings direct into the 5 inch and 6 inch pots, as it saves labour, and stronger, sturdier plants are usually obtained. [A growbag would also be suitable.]

Aftercare in the form of watering and support is vital. Interestingly Miller, Cobbett and Thompson give much attention to the growing medium but they make no mention of feeding. However, it is worth remembering that watering for them was from the mineral-rich water tanks, wells and streams rather than the tap. Today we tend to use proprietary soil-less compost which needs supplementary feeds during the growing season. Miller includes a note on ornamental kitchen style: 'In May these Plants should be transplanted, either into Pots filled with rich light Earth, or into the borders of the Flower-garden, observing to water and shade them until they have taken Root; and as the Branches are extended, they should be supported with Sticks; otherwise, when the Fruit begins to grow, it will press them down, and break them.'

He continues: 'Those Plants which are placed in Pots, should be often watered, otherwise they will come to little; for they are very droughty Plants: but when they are planted in a rich moist Soil, they will grow to a prodigious Size, and produce large Quantities of Fruit; which in Autumn, when they are ripe, make an odd Figure; but the Plants emit so strong an Effluvium, as renders them unfit to stand near an Habitation, or any Place that is much frequented; for upon their being brushed by the Cloaths, the send forth a very strong disagreeable Scent.' Watering should also be consistent, as too much variation causes the tomatoes to split.

South-facing walls provide ideal conditions for tomatoes and Cobbett suggests: 'If close to a wall, their runners may be trained up it by the means of shreds when the leaves and fruit make a very beautiful appearance. If not close to a wall, there must be sticks put to train the vines up and to tie them to. The ground in which they are planted should be kept very clean, and frequently stirred about them. If you intend to save the seed, you should have a plant or two very early placed against a south wall.' In the 1950s and '60s our local sewage farm sold the tomato seedlings that occurred 'naturally' during the processing; Japanese prisoners of war, if based anywhere long enough, tried to raise tomatoes by similar methods.

Thompson's detailed instructions continue: 'Towards the end of May the first bunch of bloom will be showing, when the plants may be hardened off ready for their fruiting quarters. If they can be got out well in advance of this first flowering there is a chance of a good set being

Fig. 1108.—Neglected Plant—side-shoots not removed.   Fig. 1109.—Result of timely removal of all superfluous growth.   Fig. 1110.—Common example of reckless defoliating.   Fig. 1111.—Tomato Plant, partially defoliated.

Tomatoes described with moral rectitude (from left to right): neglected plant – side shoots not removed; result of timely removal of all superfluous growth; common example of reckless defoliating; tomato plant, partially defoliated.

effected, whereas when raised earlier in the season and half starved, the first flowers drop prematurely, and a late crop is the consequence. Blank spaces on walls between Peach and other trees are suitable positions for Tomatoes … Those to be trained against walls and fences should be planted 1 foot apart and kept confined to a single stem, but if plants are scarce they may be arranged 3 feet, or rather less, apart, and two side-growths be laid in addition to the central one.' Estimate how tall they are going to grow and cut a piece of string a little longer; then as you plant, tuck the end of the string under the roots. Once each plant is established unfurl the string and attach it to the wall or greenhouse roof. Thompson scotches the commonly held belief that you should remove leaves as well as side shoots: 'When the fruits are approaching maturity, ripening will not be hastened by the complete removal of the leaves about them.'

Green tomatoes will ripen if placed in the dark wrapped in tissue paper, or they are delicious fried.

CAPSICUMS

Capsicums, also in the *Solanaceae* family, include sweet and chilli peppers, from which we get the powdered forms chilli, cayenne and paprika. Wild chillies were possibly eaten in Mexico from as early as 7000 BC and were certainly under cultivation by 5000 BC in South America at the time of the European Iron Age. Named by Christopher Columbus, chillies arrived in England around 1548; Gerard describes them as being 'very well knowne in the shoppes at Billingsgate by the name of Ginnie pepper'.

Miller lists eighteen varieties of capsicum or 'Guiney Pepper' and says of them: 'These sorts of Capsicums are sown in many curious Gardens with other annual Plants, in Hot-beds, and require to be treated after the same manner as was directed for the Amaranthus; and do, in the Autumn Season, make a very pretty diversity, being intermixed therewith.'

Cobbett had lived and worked in the United States, where he observed carefully the growing methods of a wide variety of fruit, vegetables and ornamental plants. He drew on that experience when he wrote *The American Gardener*, published in 1821, which he adapted for the English market as *The English Gardener* (1829), in which he writes:

Capsicum This is a plant of a hot country. It is sowed in the natural ground of the United States of America, though it is a native of

countries which are never cold. The seed is, in this country, sowed in
a gentle hot-bed, in the month of March. In the middle of April they
may be moved out, and planted under a warm wall, so as to be covered
by a frame and lights or by hand-glasses, and so as to have air given
them in the warm part of the day. When no more frost is to be expected,
and when the general earth becomes warm, that is to say about the
third week in June, the plants, very carefully taken up, and with the
earth not much shaken off from their roots, should be transplanted in
a bed of fine rich earth; but still in a warm part of the garden. The bed
should have hoops placed over it; the plants should be shaded by mats
every day for about a week, if the sun be hot; [if the beds are well
watered opaque plastic would serve instead] and if the nights be very
cold afterwards, the beds should have a little shelter in the night for a
fortnight or three weeks. To cause your plants to be very stocky and
strong, take them when in rough leaf, and prick them out on a gentle
heat, or even, if in small quantity, pot them singly, and plant them out
when you find them strong and the weather hot. In this manner one
plant will bear more fruit than a dozen little spindling ones. The plants
will be in bloom in July, and, in the month of October, their pods,
which have a strong peppery taste, would be fit to gather for pickling.
There are several sorts of the capsicum, some with red pods, some
with green ones; I do not know which is the best in quality; and a very
small quantity of these plants will suffice for any family.

Peppers are green when unripe, ripening to red, yellow or cream.
Beeton's advice in his *New Dictionary of Every-Day Gardening* is concise
and accurate:

Capsicums. Pretty ornamental plants, especially in autumn, when
covered with their light scarlet fruit. From the capsicum cayenne
pepper is made.

Preparation of the Soil. These thrive best in a rich, yet light and
free soil; and whether grown in pots or planted out, the soil should be
of this description.

Time and Manner of Sowing. The seed should be sown early in
March in well-drained pots filled with light sandy soil, and place in a
cucumber-frame, or wherever a temperature of about 65° is

maintained. Cover the seed to the depth of about half an inch, and keep the surface constantly moist [but not waterlogged] until the plants appear. When the plants are strong enough to handle, pot them off, placing two or three plants in a 5 inch pot, and replacing them in the warmth. Keep them rather close until they become established, then shift into 7 inch pots; and when they are fairly established in these, remove them, if intended for the open ground, to a cold frame, and gradually prepare them for planting out by a freer exposure to the air … They must be liberally watered during hot, dry weather. In favoured localities most of the varieties do better planted out than when grown in pots under glass; but they will not succeed in the open air except in warm, dry situations.

William Robinson has a little to add on capsicums in *The Vegetable Garden*: 'A light, rich soil, composed of turfy loam, rotted leaf-mould, and cow-manure in equal parts, with a little silver sand added, is best suited to them; but when grown and fruited in pots, a more solid soil will be found best. Well ripened pods of Capsicums will keep good for several years if placed on a dry shelf, and the seed will germinate at six or seven years old if kept in the pods until it is sown.'

He goes on to list twenty-seven varieties, some of which have names – 'Improved Bull-nose, Monstrous, Elephant's Trunk, American Bonnet, Celestial and Procopp's Giant' – that could be those of pantomime characters.

Pleasure

Bulbs

> If of thy mortal goods thou art bereft
> And of thy meagre store
> Two loaves alone to thee are left
> Sell one, and with the dole
> Buy hyacinths to feed thy soul.

Sheikh Muslih-uddin Saadi Shirazi, *The Gulista of Saadi* (1270)

Bulbs such as hyacinths, tulips, crown imperials and narcissus transformed late sixteenth-century gardens with a voluptuous enthusiasm that we still enjoy. Before then the choice of flowers for gardeners was less colourful and more aromatic, such as those John Gardener lists in *The Feate of Gardening* of *c.* 1440: 'Herbes for Savour and beaute Gyllofr gentyle, Mageron gentyle, Basyle, Palma Christi, Stycadose, Meloncez, Arcachaffe, Scalaceley, Philyppendula, Popyroyall, Germaundr', Cowsloppus of Jerusalem, Verveyn, Dyll, Seynt Mar'Garlek' – clove pinks, sweet marjoram, basil, castor oil plant, French lavender, achillea, artichoke?, mustard?, filipendula or meadowsweet, pennyroyal, germander, cowslips, vervain, dill, marguerites.

In *How to Enjoy Garden Flowers* (1928) Marcus Woodward introduces the reader to the poetry and history of hyacinths and other bulbs: 'The hyacinth is hieroglyphical of play, since it sprang from the blood of the god killed by Apollo's quoit. It seems probable that many choice hyacinth bulbs and other eastern plants were brought to this country in the reign of Elizabeth as a result of trading expeditions, such as one she authorised in 1561, visiting Persia in quest of silk.'

Hyacinths get a good press, Sam Beeton's comments in his *Shilling Gardening Book* being typical of many writers' views: 'The Hyacinth is a most delightful and valuable flower. In the conservatory or sitting-room it is equally at home, and its well-being is less dependent upon the mysteries of the gardening art and the pure atmosphere of the country than that of almost any other exotic in cultivation.'

Hyacinths can suffer from a municipal bedding image, but in *The English Flower Garden* (1883) William Robinson suggests naturalizing them in the garden: 'The familiar garden Hyacinth is not generally included among hardy plants, though it is perfectly hardy, and when treated as it should be, most important. The parent of all the varieties, H. orientalis is as hardy as a Daffodil, and its varieties are scarcely less hardy.' Beeton plants them out as well: 'If the soil be light or medium, it simply requires to be deeply dug and well worked; if heavy, besides deep digging and well working, the bulbs should be surrounded with sand, or, better still two good handfuls of cocoa [sic] fibre.' Surrounding any bulb with sharp sand is a good tip and coco-fibre is now readily available again.

The fortunes of the tulip have been well documented. Their regimented planting was greatly improved by Arts and Crafts gardeners such as Gertrude Jekyll who dispensed with serried ranks and planted them with soft clouds of forget-me-nots and other spring flowers. Her methods of drifting colour effects are beautifully outlined in *Colour Schemes for the Flower Garden* (1914), in which her description of her spring garden is like an Edwardian version of Botticelli's spring: 'Further along, just clear of the nuts, are some patches of Dicentra spectabilis, its graceful growth arching out over the lower stature of pink tulips and harmonising charmingly with the pinkish-green foliage of the tree peonies just behind. The pink tulips are here in some quantity; they run boldly into pools of pale blue Myosotis, with more Iberis where the picture demands the strongest, deepest green, and more Corydalis where the softer, greyer tones will make it better.'

In *The English Flower Garden* Robinson writes: 'Tulips are easily grown in the rich soil of old gardens, but where the land is cold and stiff or not well worked they have a tendency to die out. They may be planted from October to the middle of November, and the old Tulip growers used to put a little sand at the base of each bulb, but this is not essential. It is well to lift the bulbs every two or three years, or they become crowded and give small flowers.' Ever one to minimize unnecessary work, at a time when tulips were routinely lifted annually after flowering and replanted in the autumn, he adds that 'nothing is gained by keeping them out of the ground'.

The exacting standards of eighteenth- and nineteenth-century florists' societies dominated the exhibition of hyacinth and tulips, as well as auriculas, polyanthus, anemones, ranunculus, pinks and carnations, encouraging growers to produce flawless examples. One of the formulators of the

desirable properties of florists' flowers was George Glenny. He despaired of the hyacinth but hoped that it might be improved with 'petals broad, thick, blunt at the end, not pointed, which reflex enough to throw up the centre well'. He topped his pomposity in *The Floricultural Cabinet* (1848), in which he writes:

> I beg to call the attention of the readers to the simple fact that no writer on the Tulip ever hinted a word as to the form being circular or globular in any proportion whatever ... until I in 1832, and often since that period, laid down as a principle, that the form should be from one-third to one-half of a hollow ball ... When those writers who found their credit upon what they purloin from others have been forgotten, my standard will remain as mine and mine only ... I consider all the miserable attempts to describe the same proportions in different words very contemptible, and such is the opinion of the leading enthusiasts in floriculture.

For John Parkinson the crown imperial was the best of bulbs and he opens his *Paradisi in Sole Paradisus Terrestris* (1629) (which he dedicated to the 'Rose and Lily' queen, Henrietta Maria, wife of Charles I) with the crown

ABOVE *An auricula theatre of c. 1910, a platform for seasonal shows of plants such as primulas or geraniums.*

imperial (*Fritillaria imperialis*), saying, 'its stately beautifulnesse deserveth the first place in this our garden of delight, to be here entreated of before all other Lillies'. Suttons & Sons also note its stateliness, describing it as 'A noble plant', and adding on a practical note that these plants need 'a deep, rich moist soil, and an open situation, to ensure the full degree of stateliness ... They should be planted in autumn eighteen inches apart, allowing from four to six inches of soil above the crown.' They are then best left, as they release an unpleasant odour when picked or moved.

Like many other plants, the lily (*Lilium candidum*) was spread across Europe by the Romans as it was part of their *materia medica*. It was only with the introduction of many Oriental lilies in the late nineteenth and early twentieth centuries that what had been plain lily became the Madonna lily. Her tall stems and white flowers became a symbol of purity and Marian worship. In *Hortulus*, of *c.* AD 840, Walafrid Strabo writes: 'In this flower lies Chastity, strong in her sacred honour. If no unclean hand disturbs her, if no illicit passion does violence to her, the flower smells sweetly. But should her pride of innocence be lost, the scent turns foul and noisome.'

The fourth-century Roman writer Palladius (Rutilius Taurus Aemilianus Palladius), whose work on husbandry was translated by medieval monks, includes planting lilies in his tips for February, although in England it would be wiser to plant them in March or even early April:

> ... Now lily bulbes sow
> Or set, and them that of rather grow.
> In weeding them thou must be diligent
> For hurting of their bulb, or of their eye.
> But bulbes small up from their mother hent
> Let put in other land to multiply.

In other words, plant out and weed your Madonna lily with care and if there are any small bulblets, remove them and grow on separately.

Of another popular bulb, the narcissus or daffodil, Woodward writes: 'For hundreds of years the daffodils have taken the winds of March; they rank among the very oldest garden favourites'; and Robinson says in *The English Flower Garden*: 'They are to the spring what Roses, Irises, and Lilies are to summer, what Sunflowers and Chrysanthemums are to autumn, and what Hellebores and Aconite are to winter.' He goes on to say: 'in

naturalising the Daffodil ... do not begin as late as November or December by planting the sweepings out of the bulb-stores, since such bulbs are weak and flabby, and are liable to rot in the frozen ground. The time to begin planting is June and July, and it is a good rule to refuse to plant in quantity after August or September.' It would be interesting to try out his June and July suggestion but the rains of late September, or later if the ground is bone hard, make ideal conditions for planting out daffodils.

John Claudius Loudon designed both his house and gardens at Porchester Terrace in Bayswater in 1823 – a 'double detached villa' that cost £5,000 with a southerly aspect. In the gardens, which were a practical inspiration for their many books, he and Jane introduced 2,000 different plants, including seaweeds, mosses, and an alpine house with 600 species in pots. He introduced bulbs in the lawn some sixty years before William Robinson began encouraging gardeners to do so through his columns in *The Garden*.

Beds and borders

BORDERS

Timothy Nourse was an early exponent of year-round colour. In *Campania Foelix*, which was published posthumously in 1700, he writes: 'The Borders which may be made, more or fewer, wider or narrower, according to the Genius of the Gardner, I would have replenished with Flowers, for every Month or Season of the Year: For to see a Flower-Garden without its decorations, is all one as to sit down to a Table furnisht with Cloth, Plates and Napkin, and nothing serv'd in. To enumerate the particular Flowers would be too tedious, the Curious may find Varieties to entertain themselves ...'

ABOVE *Increasingly, as the nineteenth century drew to a close, trumpet daffodils were planted in swathes in grass.* OVERLEAF *As Victorian cities grew, so did pride in every garden detail.*

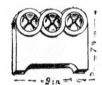

Although the task of refreshing the borders in order to maintain visual impact has been eased over the centuries, with many plant introductions increasing the amount of plants available, as the Reverend Henry Burgess points out in *The Amateur Gardener's Year-Book* (1854): 'The grand obstacle in the way of a well-filled flower garden is the want of foresight on the part of its owner. A Gardener should have the wants of his borders at every season present to his mind at any time.' He also comments: 'What are called fanciers are sad hands in this way, since they too often neglect the general appearance of their gardens. Caring for nothing but concentrated beauty, in the form of a Tulip bed or a collection of Picotees, when these favourites are withdrawn, their domains are as innocent of verdure as an Arabian Desert.'

Gertrude Jekyll has much to say that is useful on the subject of borders in *Colour in the Flower Garden* (1908). However many gardeners would draw the line at her suggestion under 'Things worth doing': 'It always seems to me that one of the things most worth doing about a garden is to try to make every part of it beautiful; not the pleasure garden only, but some of the rougher accessories also, so that no place is unsightly. For the faggot-stack can be covered with ... quick growing rambling things like the wild Bindweed (Convolvulus), or the garden variety with still larger bloom.' But you might consider growing a gourd or *Lablab purpurea* in such a spot.

George Glenny's confidently (and long-windedly) titled *The Gardener's Every-Day Book containing Plain Instructions for the Cultivation of all Classes of Flowers, Fruit and Vegetables, and the Practical Management of Every Department of Horticulture and Floriculture* of 1863 contains this simple and effective tip: 'Mignonette seed sprinkled over the great borders among the shrubs makes a very interesting weed, on account of its rich perfume.' Twenty years later Robinson pontificates on growing this plant:

Reseda (Mignonette) The only species worth growing is R. odorata and its varieties. Seed sown in the open ground in March or April produces in a few weeks flowering plants, which continue to bloom till late in autumn. If fine masses be wished for, the seed should be sown in pans about the end of March, the seedlings placed singly in 3 inch pots, and planted out in good soil in an open position. A little attention should be given to thinning out the weak shoots and stopping the vigorous ones. Plants sown in autumn will survive mild winters and produce flowers in early summer, these being finer than those of spring-sown plants.

The problem today is finding a fragrant mignonette but they are easy to raise from seed and form floriferous underplanting. Gertrude Jekyll also advised growing annuals such as sweet peas to pep up borders as they fade.

IRISES

Mrs C.W. Earle and Miss Ethel Case were two upper-class Edwardian ladies who were purveyors of advice not only on gardening but also running a household. Mrs Earle published a series of *Pot-Pourri* books inspired by her Surrey house and garden, and others with Miss Case, including *Pot-Pourri Mixed by Two* (1917), in which she expresses her dislike of flowerbeds in lawns. 'I cannot get over a strong prejudice against round and oval beds cut in grass, they belong to a period in gardening that I for one would like to see done away with, more entirely than it is; they are annually filled with bulbs and forget-me-nots in spring and tender plants in the summer.' What a shame she had not visited Jekyll's garden at Munstead Wood to see the effect of bulbs planted in freer style. 'Flowering shrubs, used as specimens, are, I think a more satisfactory way of breaking up a lawn than the old conventional beds,' Mrs Earle writes. However, she makes an exception: 'A small round bed, filled with one kind of iris, looks well if the soil is strong enough to make the leaves handsome after the flower is over.'

For soil to be 'strong' in this way it needs to be well drained and with a sunny aspect. The silver and gold variegated-leaved irises, *Iris pallida* 'Argentea' and *I.p.* 'Aurea' look sensational in such a setting. With clever manipulation you might be able to produce the ladies' horror of (early) tulips and forget-me-nots to precede the variegated iris, thus extending and varying the flowering interest. Today we also have the variety *I.* 'Gerald Derby', whose leaf base is richly coloured blue and purple.

Mrs Earle mentions an iris that she says is easy to cultivate. 'At the seaside, at the end of April, all the small gardens were filled with the dark-blue early iris, which is almost a wild plant in the south of France and at Aix-les-Bains. The nurseryman seldom sells this kind, but it is worth having, for it flowers early and, as a rule, profusely. The next easiest of cultivation is a white one …' I assume these are the tiny *Iris reticulata* available in many shades from white through to the deepest purple.

Later, talking about irises in the border, she writes: 'If you wish to increase irises, they are best moved during the summer.' Lift after three to four years, once the clump becomes crowded, and separate into single rhizomes, ensuring that you discard the central portion that has no leaves. When you replant, arrange the rhizomes so that their noses are together. At the Fondation Claude Monet at Giverny, the gardeners do this with the irises every year to ensure the Impressionistic display.

Monet regularly ordered plants from Kelway's, who bred the Intermediate bearded irises known as Langports. When these are planted *en masse* the three upstanding petals, the standards, and the three lower petals, the falls, catch and reflect the light – a reminder that the iris is named for Juno's messenger, Iris, daughter of Electra and Thaumis, who slid down the rainbow to bring messages from the gods to earth.

DIANTHUS

The name dianthus comes from the Greek *dios* and *anthos* meaning flower of the gods. The genus includes pinks, carnations and sweet Williams. In the 1630s Sir Henry Wotton, Provost of Eton College, wrote in a letter to Thomas Johnson: 'Tell me where I may have for my monye, all kinds of coloured Pynkes, to sett in a Quarter of my Garden or any such flowers as perfume the Ayre.' Carnations and pinks often have a heady clove scent, and as with roses it is a shame to grow ones without scent. Their heady clove

scent led to the old name Philip Miller uses in his description of the genus in *The Gardener's Dictionary* (third edition 1748):

Caryophyllus; Clove-gilliflower, or Carnation. The Characters are; It hath an intire, oblong, cylindrical, smooth Cup, which is indented at the Top: the Petals of the Flower are narrow at Bottom, and broad at the Top, and are for the most part laciniated, or

'Look at the carnations which you gave me.' These flowers were a suitable delight for ladies.

cut about the Edges: the Seed vessel is of a cylindrical Figure, containing many flat rough seeds.

This Genus may be divided into three Classes, for the better explaining them to Persons unacquainted with Botany; which also will be a necessary for the right understanding their Culture.

1. Caryophyllus hortensis. The Clove-gilliflower, or Carnation.

2. Caryophyllus tenuifolius plumarius; or Pink

3. Caryophyllus barbatus or Sweet-William

I shall treat of these three Classes singly, that I may the better explain their several Methods of Culture: and, first, I shall begin with the Carnation or Clove-gilliflower. These the Florists distinguish again into four Classes ... flakes ... Bizars ... Piquettes ... and ... Painted Ladies; these have their Petals of a red or purple Colour on the Upperside, and are white underneath.

The nurseryman John Rea in his 1665 *Flora* and over two hundred years later William Robinson in *The English Flower Garden* put carnations at the top of their flower lists. Rea:

> For various colours Tulips most excell,
> And some Anemonies do please as well,
> Ranunculus in richest Scarlet shine,
> And bears-ears may with these in beauty joyne,
> But yet if ask and have were in my power,
> Next to the Rose give me the Gilliflower.

And more dogmatically, Robinson:

The flowers of our own latitudes, when they are beautiful, are entitled to the first place in our gardens, and among these flowers, after the Rose, should come the Carnation, in all its brilliancy of colour, where the soil and climate are fitted for it, as is the case over a large area of our sea-girt land. It is not enough that the laced, flaked, and other varieties of Carnation should be grown in frames or otherwise; we should show the flower in all its force of colour in our flower gardens. Many who have not the skill, or the time, for the growth of the 'florists' flower, would yet find the brilliant 'self' Carnations delightful

in their gardens in summer and autumn, and even in winter, for the
Carnation, where it does well, has a fine colour-value of foliage in
winter, which makes it most useful to all who care for colour in their
gardens, adorning the garden throughout the winter and spring, and full
of promise for the summer and autumn.

Behind the florists' plates of this century we have the pictures of the
Dutch flower painters containing fine Carnations, well grown and
admirably drawn after nature. These artists were not confused by any
false ideal, and so we have a true record of what the Carnation was three
hundred years ago. In these pictures we generally see the finer striped
and flaked kinds given the first place, which is natural, as such varieties
are apt to strike people the most; and in those days little consideration
had yet been given to the question of effect in open gardens. In our own
day this question has been forced upon us in very unpleasant ways by
masses of crudely arranged, and not always pretty flowers.

Shrubs and climbers

The way you plant a tree or shrub is critical to its success, as the Reverend
Henry Burgess observes in *The Amateur Gardener's Year-Book* (1854): 'Reader,
did you ever see a tender mother soothe a child to sleep, and afterwards lay
it down to rest? ... An experienced eye can tell whether a proper degree of
repose (so to speak) is given to a plant when committed to the earth, and
from the way in which this is done, can predict the future destiny of the
shrub or tree ... To dig a hole, and thrust the roots into it; and afterwards
tread down the loosened soil is, with many, the whole theory and practice
of planting.' And if you are squeezing one more shrub into a border, it is
better to trim back the newcomer's roots, so that it can grow into the space,
than to cram and squash, effectively creating a pot-bound shrub before it
even starts to grow.

Cobbett understands the value of giving a tree or shrub a good start. In
The English Gardener, he says: 'The hole must be much deeper and wider than
is required for the mere reception of the root. The earth ought to be broken
very finely at the bottom of the hole ... very fine earth should be put upon
the roots: if it were sifted, so much the better: the tree should be joggled or
shaken a little, to cause the earth to go down in and amongst the roots and
fill up all the cavities, so that the fine earth may touch the roots, and lie

closely round them in every part. If you tumble in the rough earth, which would leave part of the roots untouched, the parts so untouched will mould, will perish, or become cankered.' This is because root hairs cannot take up moisture unless they are in direct contact with the earth. At this stage you could also dig in some compost – it is worth investing in some if you do not have your own supply. Cobbett continues: 'When the roots are all covered with very fine earth, you may fill up the hole with the earth that has come out of it, only taking care to break it very fine … give a gentle tread all round the tree with your foot … put the rest of the earth over the treading, and leave the surface round the treading in the form of a dish.' Treading, taking care not to compact the soil, ensures that the earth is tucked all around the roots and a dish-shaped compression around the stem of the plant will stop water (either rain or irrigation) from running away before percolating through into the area around the plant.

Once a tree or shrub is planted, mulching can help retain warmth and moisture, by slowing down evaporation, and stop soil erosion, as described by Virgil: 'I have even found some who loaded heavy fieldstones on top or considerable weights of broken pots; this is protection against cloudbursts and against the hot summer heat which cracks the thirsty fields.' Columella

ABOVE *The caption to this illustration is 'Love in a Garden'. Sleeves rolled up but unbending in her whalebone corset, the lady appears to be instructing her lover on the art of tree planting.*

recommends stone mulching for grapes and apricots.

Rosemary is a shrub that has been grown in gardens for hundreds of years. It is described in Book LXXXI of the Saxon *Herbarium of Apuleis* – 'This wort, which is named rosemary, and by another name bothen, is produced on sandy lands and on wort beds' – with its uses. Sir Thomas More grew it when he lived at Chelsea Manor in the sixteenth century: 'As for Rosemarine, I lett it runne all over my garden walls, not onlie because my bees love it, but because it is the herb sacred to remembrance, and, therefore, to friendship; whence a sprig of it hath a dumb language that maketh it the chosen emblem of our funeral wakes and in our buriall grounds.'

Gertrude Jekyll describes the pleasure of growing it in *Home and Garden* (1900): 'I plant rosemary all over the garden, so pleasant is it to know that at every few steps one may draw the kindly branchlets through one's hand, and have the enjoyment of their incomparable incense; and I grow it against walls, so that the sun may draw out its inexhaustible sweetness to greet me as I pass; and early in March, before any other scented flower of evergreen is out, it gladdens me with the thick setting of pretty lavender-grey bloom crowding all along the leafy spikes.' And in *Wood and Garden* a year earlier: 'In the narrow border at the foot of the wall is a bush of Raphiolepis ovata, always to me an interesting shrub, with its thick, roundish, leathery leaves and white flower-clusters, also bushes of rosemary, some just filling the border and some trained up the wall. Our Tudor ancestors were fond of rosemary-covered walls, and I have seen old bushes quite ten feet high on the garden walls of Italian monasteries. Among the rosemaries I always like, if possible, to 'tickle in' a china Rose or two, the tender pink of the rose seems to go so well with dark but dull-surfaced rosemary.'

Raphiolepis ovata (now *Rhapiolepis umbellate*) or Japanese hawthorn is a sturdy, fragrant, handsome evergreen whose flowers are reminiscent of apple blossom. Like the rosemary it thrives in full sun – in fact it becomes lax and untidy in the slightest shade – and is an excellent wall shrub. Robinson describes it as 'a beautiful Japanese shrub, hardy in southern districts, and with a little winter protection may even be planted in cold parts. Its thick evergreen leaves are of a dark colour, and its flowers, which are large, white, and sweet-scented, are in clusters terminating the young branches.'

Flowering shrubs and climbers planted in and around trees became the vogue in the eighteenth century when the landscape movement swept away the parterres and flowerbeds of the formal garden in favour of a more

informal 'natural' style of meadows, contoured hills and clumps of trees.
One such landscape was Claremont in Surrey. The dramatist John
Vanbrugh bought Chargate farm, whose situation was 'singularly romantik',
and built a belvedere; then in 1713 he sold out to Thomas Pelham-Holles,
who became Earl of Clare, later Duke of Newcastle and Prime Minister,
and developed the property with Vanbrugh as architect, renaming it
Claremont. A guest in May 1763 evocatively describes an evening there:

> We walked to the belvedere on the summit of the hill, where
> a theatrical show only served to heighten the beauty of the landscape,
> a rainbow on a dark cloud falling precisely behind the tower of a
> neighbouring church, and the building at Claremont ... From thence
> we passed into the wood, and the ladies formed a circle on chairs
> before the mouth of a cave, which was overhung to a vast height with
> woodbines, lilacs and laburnums, and dignified with tall stately
> cypresses. On the descent of the hill were placed French horns; the
> abigails, servants and neighbours wandering below by the river; in
> short, it was Parnassus, as Watteau would have painted it.

The scene recalls Tennyson's wait at the garden gate for Maud, when
'the spice of the woodbine wafts abroad and the musk of rose is blown'.

Henry A. Bright writes of a shrub to be enjoyed in the evening in *A Year
in a Lancashire Garden* (1901):

> On a patch of green grass near the house stands a Yucca gloriosa,
> which I am always hoping will flower, but it has never done so yet. Not
> long ago I was at a stately place in Shropshire and at the end of a broad
> walk, where a circle of Yuccas had been planted, there were no less
> than five in full flower, throwing up pale jets of blossom, like
> fountains, towards the sky. I never saw anything more perfect in its
> way. But it is said that the right time to see a Yucca is by moonlight.
> There is a very striking passage in one of the letters of the most
> remarkable of American women, Margaret Fuller (afterwards
> Countess D'Ossoli) ... 'This flower was made for the moon as the
> Heliotrope is for the sun, and refuses other influences, or to display
> her beauty in any other light ... these transparent leaves of greenish
> white, which look dull in the day are melted by the moon to glistening

silver...' The second evening I went out into the garden again. In clearest moonlight stood my flower, more beautiful than ever. The stalk pierced the air like a spear; all the bells had erected themselves around it in most graceful array with petals more transparent than silver, and of softer light than the diamond. Their edges were clearly but not sharply defined – they seemed fringed by most delicate gossamer, and the plant might claim, with pride, its distinctive epithet of filamentosa.

Jekyll and Robinson both favoured the architectural and statuesque qualities of the yucca introduced to England from North America. Robinson describes it in *The English Flower Garden*: 'Yucca (Adam's Needle). – Very distinct evergreen plants of fine form and of value where effect is sought. They are hardy for the most part, and all of the kinds mentioned are vigorous but not so good on cold soils. The free-flowering kinds, Y. filamentosa and Y. flaccida, may be associated with any of our nobler autumn-flowering plants. Even species that do not flower so often, like Y. pendula and Y. gloriosa, are fine if grown in the full sun and in good soil.' He particularly likes *Y. gloriosa*: 'A large and imposing Yucca of distinct habit and somewhat rigid aspect. Its flower-stem is over 7 feet high, much branched, and bears an immense pyramidal panicle of large almost white flowers. Its numerous leaves are stiff and pointed. It is one of the noblest plants in our gardens, suitable for almost any position. In many gardens of proved hardiness.'

Roses

SAY IT WITH ROSES

A label displaying British pride. The grower added the assurance that 'Bees Ltd affix their YELLOW Trade Mark Seal to every rose tree they send out'.

The different colours, types and stages of roses provide at least fourteen different meanings for the initiated. John Boyle O'Reilly's Victorian poem 'A White Rose' must surely be amongst the most sensual:

> The red rose whispers of passion,
> And the white rose breathes of love;
> O, the red rose is a falcon,
> And the white rose is a dove.
> But I send you a cream-white rosebud
> With a flush on its petal tips;
> For the love that is purest and sweetest
> Has a kiss of desire on the lips.

As the flower of love the rose has roots in many cultures. It has been said, for instance, that it represents the mythological love of Venus or Cupid, the pure love of the Virgin Mary and the sanctity of Muhammad. There is a Romanian tradition that a beautiful princess bathing in the sea dazzled the sun with her radiance. The sun stopped in his tracks to gaze, and his fervent kisses turned her into a rose. To this day the flower hangs her head and blushes whenever the sun is too bright.

BEST ROSES

The Rose is not only 'decorative' but is the queen of all decorative plants, not in one sort of garden, but in many – not in one race or sort, but in many, from Anna Olivier, Edith Gifford and Tea Roses of that noble type in the heart of the choicest flower garden, to the wild Rose that tosses its long arms from the hedgerows in the rich soils of midland England, and the climbing Roses in their many forms. And fine as the old climbing Roses were, we have now a far nobler race of climbing Teas which, in addition to the highest beauty, have the great quality of flowering, like Bouquet d'Or, throughout the fine summer and late into the autumn.

The outcome of it all is that the Rose must go back to the flower garden – its true place, not only for its own sake, but to save the garden from ugliness, and to give it fragrance and beauty of leaf and flower.

Two of the roses William Robinson mentions are still obtainable today, both introduced in 1872. 'Anna Olivier' is a scented Tea rose whose soft primrose-coloured flowers are continuous and well perfumed; it can be grown in a tub. 'Bouquet d'Or' is a repeat-flowering Noisette rose, slightly scented with coppery-salmon and yellow-centred flowers.

Robinson was not alone in his enthusiasm for roses. The voluptuous softness of roses filled many corners of Gertrude Jekyll's garden at Munstead Wood. In *Colour Schemes for the Flower Garden* (1914) she describes some of them:

> One of the joys of June is the beauty of the Burnet roses. On the south side of the house there are figs and vines, rosemary and China roses, then a path, from which easy stone steps lead up to the strip of lawn some fifty feet wide that skirts the wood. To right and left of the steps, for a length equal to that of the house-front, is a hedge of these charming little roses. They are mostly double white, but some are rosy and some yellow. When it is not in flower the mass of small foliage is pleasant to see, and even in winter leaflessness the tangle of close-locked branches has an appearance of warm brown comfort that makes it good to have near a house.
>
> ... for the early days of July there are clumps of the old garden roses – Damask and Provence. The whole south-western angle is occupied by a well-grown 'Garland' rose that every summer is loaded with its graceful wreaths of bloom. It has never been trained or staked but grows as a natural fountain; the branches are neither pruned nor shortened. The only attention it receives is that every three or four years the internal mass of old dead wood is cut right out, when the bush seems to spring into new life.

Doing this also ensures that the fragrant, small, semi-double creamy-white flowers blossom from top to bottom, not just as an upper frill. She continues:

> Passing this angle and going along the path leading to the studio door in the little stone-paved court, there is a seat under an arbour formed by the yews; the front of it has a rambler rose, 'Sanders' White Rambler', supported by a rough wooden framework. On the right, next the paving, are two large standard roses with heads three and four

feet through. They are old garden roses, worked in cottage fashion on a common dog-rose stock. One is 'Céleste', of loveliest tender rose colour, its broad bluish leaves showing its near relationship to Rosa alba; the other the white 'Mme Plantier'. This old rose, with its abundant bunches of pure white flowers, always seems to me to be one of the most charming of the older garden kinds. It will grow in almost any way, and is delightful in all; as a pillar, as a hedge, as a bush, as a big cottage standard, or in the border tumbling about among early summer flowers. Like the 'Blush Damask', which just precedes it in quantity in every garden, and yet they are but rarely to be seen.

Just as Jekyll's words make you want to run out with your shopping list – and the varieties she names are all still available – Thomas Hill would have appealed to the Tudor garden dreamer when in *The Gardener's Labyrinth* (1577) he writes: 'Roses are of several sorts and Colours, as White, Red, Damask, Province, Musk and Sweet-bryer, etc. Of all the flowers in the Garden, this is the chief for beauty and sweetness: Rose-trees are commonly planted in a plot by themselves, (if you have roome enough) leaving a pretty space betwixt them for gathering … Your Provast Roses wil bear the same year you set them. You may if you please, plant Strawberies, Primroses, and Violets amongst your rose-trees, and they wil prosper very wel.'

CLIMBERS AND RAMBLERS
Hill also knew about the ornamental value of training 'tumbling' musk and damask roses. He explains how to do this:

The owner or gardener that would set Rose trees to run up by the poles of the herbar, ought workmanly to begin and do the same about the middest of February, and in the first quarter of the Moon, the beds before well reared with a stony and dry earth, and not with dung. The rose trees with their roots, are also to be planted in short and narrow beds diligently raised with a dry earth … The owner also may set the Jasmine tree bearing a fragrant flower, the musk Rose, damask Rose, and Privet tree, in beds of drie earth, to shoot up and spread over this herbar, which in time growing, not only defendeth the heat of the Sun, but yieldeth a delectable smel, much refreshing the sitters under it.

When tying in roses in February, it is preferable to do so in the middle of a sunny day, when the branches will be more supple and less like to break.

Helen Crofton grew climbing roses. As well as offering the timeless advice that 'It is no use having a new Rose if it is not a good grower, and old favourites should never be discarded for new if they are strong, of good colour, and flower courageously,' she describes her preferences in *Garden Colour* (1905): 'I grow the Carmine Pillar up larch poles in my garden, and by the door of my Garden Room. It is by far the best Pillar Rose that there is, and though it sometimes loses leaves it never gets mildewed like the dear Crimson Rambler, and is a more possible colour to paint. 'Dorothy Perkins' is a lovely pink climber, but I have not yet tested its strength.' In fact Dotty P. has plenty of strength but it is a martyr to mildew.

Jekyll advocates just letting roses scramble up trees: 'The dark trees on the right have rambling roses growing into them – 'Paul's Carmine Pillar' and the Himalayan *R. brunonii*. The red rose does not flower so freely here as on a pillar in sunlight, but its fewer stems clamber high into the holly, and the bloom shows in thin natural wreaths that are even more pleasing to an artist's eye than the more ordered abundance of the flowery post.' You can grow roses up leylandii as well.

This photograph is simply entitled 'c. 1910 with Herbert'. Is Herbert the man or the dog accompanying the ladies enjoying Tennyson's 'musk of the rose'?

Margaret Waterfield also grew climbing roses, amongst many others. In *Garden Colour*, which she contributed to and illustrated, she writes about 'The Banksian Roses'. These roses were named for Joseph Banks. *Rosa banksiae* var. *banksiae* and *R.b.* 'Lutea' were introduced in 1807 and pre-1824 respectively; the later *R.b.* 'Lutescens', introduced in 1870, is the most sweetly scented. She says: '... both white and yellow, grow freely here, probably liking the dry chalk subsoil; one old white plant, now some forty feet in height, has been on the house thirty years or more. It must not be forgotten that the little pruning these Roses want must be done directly they have ceased to flower; the young growth of the year should be cut back, and weak wood taken right out.' This advice follows the usual principles of pruning, but with critical timing. All these roses are vigorous if grown in a sunny, sheltered position. She continues:

Among dwarf varieties, the China Roses are the first and also the last to bloom. They look particularly well planted in large masses, and are literally perpetual. Directly the flowers have been cut off they set to work to form new sprays, and are just as gay as ever in a week or two ... nearly all the Monthlies are worth growing, particularly: – Eugène Résal – copper and bright rose pink. Laurette Messimy – salmon pink. Comtesse du Caÿla – orange and red; gorgeous. All these are vigorous and quite lovely, and seldom without flowers. [Only 'Comtesse du Caÿla' is still commercially available.] Other good kinds are: – ... Cramoisie-supérieure – red; will climb. The free-growing Monthlies can be planted among shrubs in herbaceous borders. A tangle of Cramoisie-supérieure [still available] with Spiraea Aruncus [now *Aruncus dioicus*] and the Gum cistus is delightful. The white flowers of the Cistus glisten all the morning, but by twelve o'clock their beauty is gone, the petals fallen to the ground, and only the sprays of buds are left, with their promise for the morrow. Another good contrast of white and red can be got with this same red China Rose and double Deutsia.

The uses to which ... free growing Roses can be put are almost endless. If there is an ugly fence to cover, or a screen is wanted to separate one bit of garden from another, a few posts and a light trellis may be easily put up, and will be covered in two years with Roses. Walls, Pergolas, arches, bridges, banks of streams, etc., may all be clothed. The more naturally they are grown the better they look ...

Rose Euphrosyne with white Foxgloves shows how charmingly they can be used to form a tangle of beauty in the wild garden.

Should you wish to train your roses and climbers in a more orderly fashion, turn to Beeton's *Shilling Gardening Book*, where he describes 'TRELLIS-WORK (Making of)':

This may frequently be introduced with good effect in the mixed flower and kitchen-garden, to shut out buildings or unsightly objects. Small oak stands, or small larch poles, about five or six feet apart, and having the intervals filled with thin iron wires crossing each other, form the most durable trellis-work. Against the walls of a house a very nice trellis-work may be made with a lacing of copper wire over nails of the same. This may be worked in any pattern and carried in any direction; to this wire the creepers may be tied when necessary; and in this way the walls of houses may be covered with flowers or evergreens, without any injury to the brick-work from continual nailing.

We associate espalier and fan training with fruit but Beeton guides the gardener to do the same with roses. 'Roses, as espaliers, may be made to assume a striking feature in the economy of an ornamental rose-garden. The espaliers should be formed of galvanized iron, five feet or so high, and of proportionate width. Hurdles of this material, if the bars be close

Mrs Loudon considered training 'an important operation'. In The Amateur Gardener *(1847) she illustrates training in pots or into pyramids. Note the tiny hooks to tie the branches on to.*

enough, will answer very well; but the bars should not be more than six inches apart. This form of rose-training is especially suitable for varieties with weak footstalks, notably Maréchal Niel.' This is a highly scented, golden-yellow repeat-flowering Noisette rose, introduced in 1864, which only thrives in a greenhouse or warm sheltered position.

'The plants used should be of strong-growing habit ... and planted upon the southern aspect, or as near to that as possible,' Beeton continues. 'Intertwine and mix the branches as thickly as may be, and tie them to the cross-bars with wire or tarred string.' Note that iron heats up and can damage the rose on hot summer days unless it is completely masked. 'To construct a rose-terrace, let such espaliers as described above form the back rows of sloping beds; an ascent may thus be charmingly laid out in stages, with path and terrace alternately to the level ground.' He recommends this treatment for 'Laura Davant – pink, double; Russelliana – dark crimson, double; Madame D'Arblay – white, blooming in clusters; The Garland – nankeen [creamy-white] and pink, semi-double; Frederick the Second – rich crimson-purple; Juno – pale rose, very large; Madame Plantier – pure white; Madeline – pale flesh.' If you use the hardier 'Russelliana' (also known as 'Old Spanish Rose', 'Russell's Cottage', 'Scarlet Grevillea' and 'Souvenir de la Bataille de Marengo') 'Madame D'Arblay', 'The Garland', 'Juno' or 'Madame Plantier', note that they are summer flowering: you may want to combine them with another climber.

Beeton and Waterfield both like Ayrshire roses. Margaret Waterfield says: 'A Rose alley is a delightful sight ... Hybrids of rosa multiflora and Wichuriana, or the Ayrshire Roses, could well be used in this way.' Sam Beeton:

The rapidity with which this rose covers a wall or pillar, added to its intrinsic beauty, renders it invaluable to the gardener. Where its growth is encouraged, it climbs to the summit of the tallest trees, from which its long graceful shoots hang in festoons. The Ayrshire seems to have been first grown in the garden of the Earl of Loudon, at Loudon Castle, Ayrshire. It soon found its way into the nurseries in Scotland, whence, in 1811, it was transplanted to London by Mr. Ronalds, of Brentford ... There is more than one tradition connected with the introduction of this rose ... Whatever the truth there may be ... it is pretty certain that no rose having the slightest resemblance to the Ayrshire has since been discovered on the American continent ... The

Ayrshire is the hardiest of climbing roses, and its cultivation and management are very simple. Layers of its long pendulous shoots root readily, and it strikes easily from cuttings; it will grow rapidly where other roses will scarcely exist, and when placed in good rich soil, its growth is so rapid that a large space is covered by it in the second season of planting. It is useful for trellis, verandah, or alcove, as well as in rough places of the park or shrubbery. Its luxuriant growth soon turns a rough and dreary waste into a flowery bank.

Henry A. Bright describes a reason why climbers may fail to thrive in *A Year in a Lancashire Garden* (1901):

The Magnolia (also a Grandiflora) on the house has also begun to flower, but I had nearly lost it altogether, and the story is rather a curious one. I had noticed that both it and other creepers were looking unhappy, and I could not guess the reason. The Escallonia showed bare branches in many places, the Ceanothus seemed shrunken and brown, and a Gloire de Dijon Rose did no good. At last it occurred to my gardener that the galvanised wire, which I had put up to avoid driving nails into the stone work of the windows, was to blame. I pulled it all down, coated it thickly over with paint, and, when it was again put up, all the creepers seemed to start into fresh life, and grew strong and vigorous.

I trained the climbing tea rose 'Gloire de Dijon' directly on to a metal chain and it also failed to thrive. I have now combined it with leafier climbers, which protect it from the metal, and it flowers freely and mostly manages to repeat later in the season.

PLANTING

The great rosarian Dean Hole, writing in *Our Gardens* (1899), gave very specific advice to his readers on the best site for roses: 'The Rose Garden must not be in an exposed situation. It must have shelter, but it must not have shade. No boughs may darken, no drip may saturate, no roots may rob, the Rose. Screens there should be to resist rude Boreas, breakwaters to the haven, but not near enough to intercept the sunshine or the free circulation of air. They rejoice in that sunshine, and should have what there is to be had of it in this our cloudy land. I believe E.S.E. to be the best aspect for Roses, so manifest is the influence of the rising and midday sun.' This advice is not suitable for all roses: for instance, the beautiful, gorgeously fragrant claret-coloured Hybrid Perpetual 'Souvenir du Docteur Jamain', introduced in 1865, requires dappled shade to come to perfect flowering.

In the spirit of the 1980s advice 'spend £5 on the plant and £10 on the hole', Edwardian Rose Kingsley in *Garden Colour* argues for growing China roses 'with the same generous treatment bestowed on a Rose that costs 7s 6d instead of 9d', adding 'what a lovely object is a big plant of the old pink China, the parent of so many beautiful children'. Waterfield says much the same: 'If a good square hole were cut in the grass when they were first planted, and the soil properly made they would need very little attention for years.'

When you plant roses, Dean Hole says in *A Book About Roses* (1901), the 'union of the Rose to the stock should be about two inches below the ground'. Modern nurseries advise just one inch, but planting lower helps to prevent the rootstock from sending up suckers.

CARE

Dean Hole realized that success with rose growing depends on continual care. He recounts in the same book:

> 'I say, old fellow', remarked to me a friend as we rode together in the Row, and with a tone which, though it pretended a cheery indifference, was fraught with rebuke and anger, 'those Rose-trees, which you recommended me to get, turned out a regular do. Cost a hatful of money – precious near a tenner, if not all out – and, by Jove, sir! our curate at the county flower-show came and licked them all into fits!' 'Robert', I responded (I was too indignant to address him with Bob, as usual), 'I never in my life recommended a person of your profound ignorance to have anything to do with Roses. You asked me to give you a list of the best, and I did so reluctantly, knowing that you had neither taste nor the energy to do them justice. As to the outlay, the animal on which you have recklessly placed yourself, and whose hocks are a disgrace to this park, cost you, I know, more than eighty guineas; and for a tithe of that sum, without further supervision or effort, you expect a beautiful Rose-garden. I rejoice to hear that the curate beat you.

As we have seen earlier, Robinson is against the common practice of feeding roses with manure:

> On this day, 1st October 1919, many of the finest Roses are in good bloom. I have grown Roses here for over a quarter of a century with success and without the usual excess of manure below and on the surface, this last called mulching. It seems to me that to cover beds near the house with excreta from the farm and other yards is anything but a sanitary or even a necessary thing to do. So our rosebeds are done without it either above or below. We never mulch the beds, but cover them with beautiful plants instead. We set the Roses rather thinly and add many plants beneath them, mostly low in stature. The beds were dug deep, a base of poor shale thrown out for 3 feet. The turf on the surface was buried, and that we found to be a mistake, as it was full of grubs of daddy-long-legs and other pests, which destroyed the Carnations for two years afterwards. We ought to have burned the turf. The soil was cool loam rather heavier than I should make it now, being then misled by the catalogues, which told us that Roses must have heavy soil and heaps of manure. Now we only cover the surface with beautiful life, and practise rotation on that. For example, one year's Mignonette is followed by the Missouri Evening Primrose.

In his 'Preface to the New Edition' of *The English Flower Garden* (1933) he lists more 'living plants' that can be used instead of a mulch: 'Viola, Mignonette, Shamrock Pea, and some of the beautiful annuals of California, which, if they escape the slugs in the winter, give us very beautiful results.' He goes on: 'The next delusion is that the plants must be pruned late in the spring, April, say, so that they are left all the winter to be knocked about by storms and frosts. This habit is given as law in every Rose book, but it is a much better practice to prune all our Roses before Christmas, if possible, and set them to work to make roots.' Pruning in this way is more common today but when deciding whether to follow his advice take into account your local climate. It is probably best to prune later in colder sites. Alternatively deadheading and a bit more is a good way of continual light pruning.

FORCING

The fourth-century Roman writer Palladius includes forcing roses in his tips

for February, although in England it would be wiser to suggest March or
even April. He says:

> With craft eke roses early ripened are;
> Twain handbreadth off about their rootes do
> A delving make, and every day thereto
> Do water warm.

The modern-day equivalent would be preparing a flowerbed around the
outer drainpipes of a washing machine or dishwasher.

PROPAGATION

To propagate a rose, Thomas Hill suggests taking suckers from the root:

> Now for to get and set your plants, you must do thus, In the latter end
> of January, February, or beginning of March, (at the increase of the
> Moon,) go to some old-Rose-trees, (but not too old) and you shall find
> long young suckers or Branches, which spring up from the root of the
> tree the last year; dig a hole so deep, that you may cut away those
> Suckers close the root, (but take heed of wounding the tree,) then fill
> up the hole again with earth very close and hard; These Suckers must
> be your plants for young Trees. If the Suckers have too many branches
> cut them away, also the tops of them, and they will take root the better:
> Then where you intend to set them, dig holes in good ground at least ·
> a foot deep, and set them a good depth, treading in the earth hard
> about them, leaving a little trench neer them for watering, till they have
> taken root.

Taking cuttings is the method used more commonly today. Robinson
explains:

> The main difficulty is transplanting, the roots being more fragile than
> those of the Brier. The best way of all is to put the cuttings where the
> plants are wanted to grow, and so ensuring to them a long life. The
> best time to make cuttings of the half-ripened wood is in September,
> or, in warm valleys, a little later. Our cuttings are usually about 10
> inches long and often with a heel, and are inserted for the greater part

of their length in the freest sandy loam in the place. We began with
heavy soil, which in catalogues is said to be the best – that is because
the Brier being universally used the soil must suit it; but for the Teas
and Chinas the best soil is a free sandy loam in which the roots can
find all they need.

When taking cuttings of climbing and rambling roses, I have found
Robinson's advice that September is a good month to be sound.

Hill also suggests taking cuttings not from the rose's branches but from
its roots:

The rose trees with their roots, are also to be planted in short and
narrow beds diligently raised with a dry earth: But if the Gardener or
owner wil, slips may be broken off from the roots, cut in a slope
manner at the heads, about a mans foot and a half long, writhed at the
ends, and so set in a slope manner, a foot deep into beds, wel reared
with a drie earth, and in the increase of the Moon. The old trees new
set every fifth year in the wane of the Moon take root the sooner, and
yield the more Roses, being pruned and refreshed every year with new
and drie earth about the roots, for neither the slips nor old roots joy in
a fat clay, or moist ground, but in the drie and stony earth, and to be
set in rankes wel a foot distance one from another, in drie beds wel
reared up; for bestowed in ranks of such distance between, they
prosper the better, and yield more Roses.

For those who wish to raise roses from seed, here is Hill's advice:

... the seeds of the Rose committed to the earth, do slowly come up, yet
so often as you mind to sow the seeds, bestow them a foot deep in light
and drie earth, about the middest of March with us, and in February in
hotter places, the Moon then increasing. Here may any truly learn by the
instruction of the worthy Neapolitane Palladius Rutilius, which are the
seeds of the rose: for a man (saith he) may not think the yellow grains
with the Rose flower (being of a golden colour) to be them, but the
knobs which grow after the manner of a most short and small Pear, the
seeds of which are then ful ripe, when they be perceived brownish and
soft, which will be in the moneth of September.

ROSE RAGE

Rose pests and diseases have vexed gardeners for centuries, not least Beeton:

> There is no class of flowers so much exposed to the depredations without a precise knowledge of their habits and different states of transition. St. Pierre, when he had studied the economy of the different insects which infest the rose-tree for thirty years still found something new to note. Moths, beetles, and gall flies, and other insects hardly known to the initiated, seem to unite their forces in order to attack the queen of flowers. During June and July, the rose-beetle (Cetonia aurata) may be seen wheeling round the rose-tree, with its low hum, its wing-cases and elytra erect, instead of being extended from the body. It feeds upon pollen and honey, and in doing so bites off the anthers of the flowers, while its larvae feed upon decaying wood and vegetable matter, burying themselves in the ground like the cockchafer.

It hardly seems safe to go into the garden in June and July!

Here are some preventative tactics against some of the evils that can beset roses. Medieval Albertus Magnus advises: 'Let rue be set in many places among them, for the beauty of its green foliage and also that its biting quality may drive away noxious vermin from the garden.' *Ruta graveolens* 'Jackman's Blue' and its variegated form look especially good under pink roses. Jane Loudon suggests in *The Amateur Gardener* domestic detritus – 'greasy cabbage-leaves and heaps of brewer's grains are also good traps for slugs and snails'. Or you could try George Mount's advice of 1905 in *Garden Colour*:

> Before finishing I will give a few directions for getting rid of pests that infest the Rose. Early in Spring caterpillars may appear in the foliage and bud, and the best way to get rid of them is to pick them off and crush them. Later on green fly often appears, and that is best destroyed by a solution of soft-soap in water, just strong enough to make the water lather freely. When the solution is made, syringe the Roses in the evening and again the next evening if the first time was not sufficient to kill the green fly; it is better to syringe twice than to do it too strong the first time. Mildew often appears about the end of June; the best remedy is to dust flower of sulphur over the plant and to take off and

burn the worst leaves. Later on in the season it is almost impossible to stop mildew, and it is hardly worth while to try. Red rust is sometimes troublesome ... pick off and burn the worst leaves.

As legislation is tightened over the domestic use of pesticides, and herbicides it is worth trying old brews, such as boiled-up elder (*Sambucus* spp.) leaves, which can be syringed over roses to get rid of aphids (a tip suggested by Karen Kenny in the radio programme from which this book originated).

You could if you were desperate use Sam Beeton's 1862 recipe from his *New Dictionary of Every-Day Gardening*:

Fumigation, Easy Mode of The following simple method of fumigation is recommended ... To kill green fly on plants, take a short tobacco pipe and attach to the stem any length of indiarubber tubing the size of a feeding-bottle tube; fill the bowl three parts full of strong tobacco, light it, place a piece of muslin or flannel over the bowl, and holding the end of the pipe about 2 inches from the place affected, blow through the tube, when such a dense volume of smoke is emitted from the bowl that in the course of thirty seconds the insects will drop dead or can be shaken off. Great care should be taken that no juice falls on the foliage, or it will destroy it. ... he has used this method with complete success for years and it beats everything he is acquainted with for cheapness and effectiveness when single plants require fumigating.

Suttons & Sons of Reading write with moral vigour in their 1930s catalogue: 'Insects are among the frailest of living creatures and they perish at a touch. As they breathe through the pores of the skin, water alone – the promoter of life and cleanliness – is death to them; and they are still more subject to sure destruction when to the water is added an active poison, such as tobacco, or a substance that adheres to them and stops the process of breathing, such as glue, clay, sulphur, soft soap, and the numerous preparations that are specially made to annihilate insect hosts.'

PLANT COMMUNICATION
In 1905 Joachim Carvallo, at the château of Villandry in France, created a series of Renaissance-inspired geometric parterres, including a magnificent

potager, which can still be visited today. The sources he consulted in his researches included the Renaissance work *Monasticon Gallicanum,* which recorded that monks randomly planted rose bushes so that when they were not tending their gardens the other plants would sense that there was still someone watching over them.

The idea of plants communicating is singularly explored by Lewis Carroll in *Through the Looking Glass* (1872) when Alice steps into the Garden of Live Flowers:

This time she came upon a large flower-bed, with a border of daisies, and a willow-tree growing in the middle.

'Oh tiger-lily!' said Alice, addressing herself to one that was waving gracefully about in the wind, 'I wish you could talk!'

'We can talk,' said the Tiger-lily, 'when there's anybody worth talking to.' ...

'And can all the flowers talk?'

'As well as you can,' said the Tiger-lily. 'And a great deal louder.'

'It isn't manners for us to begin, you know,' said the Rose, 'and I really was wondering when you'd speak! Said I to myself, "Her face has got some sense in it, though it's not a clever one!" Still, you're the right colour, and that goes a long way.'

'I don't care about the colour,' the Tiger-lily remarked. 'If only her petals curled up a little more, she'd be all right.'

Alice didn't like being criticized, so she began asking questions. 'Aren't you sometimes frightened at being planted out here, with nobody to take care for you?'

'There's the tree in the middle,' said the Rose. 'What else is it good for?'

'But what could it do, if any danger came?' Alice asked.

'It could bark,' said the Rose.

'It says "Bough-wough!"' cried a Daisy. 'That's why its branches are called boughs!'

'Didn't you know that?' cried another Daisy.

And here they all began shouting together, till the air seemed quite full of little shrill voices.

'Silence, every one of you!' cried the Tiger-lily, waving itself passionately from side to side, and trembling with excitement. 'They know I can't get at them!' it panted, bending its quivering head towards Alice, 'or they wouldn't dare to do it!'

'Never mind!' Alice said in a soothing tone, and, stooping down to the daisies, who were just beginning again, she whispered, 'If you don't hold your tongues, I'll pick you!'

There was silence in a moment, and several of the pink daisies turned white …

'How is it you can all talk so nicely?' Alice said, hoping to get it [the Tiger-lily] into a better temper by a compliment. 'I've been in many gardens before, but none of the flowers could talk.'

'Put your hand down, and feel the ground,' said the Tiger-lily. 'Then you'll know why.'

Alice did so. 'It's very hard,' she said; 'but I don't see what that has to do with it.'

'In most gardens,' the Tiger-lily said, 'they make the beds too soft – so that the flowers are always asleep.'

Lawns

J.B. Papworth defines a lawn in *Hints on Ornamental Gardening* (1923): 'By the lawn is meant that portion of the grass plat which lies between the house and the pasture, which is constantly kept mown, forming a verdant carpet on which the building stands … The lawn is usually separated from the pasture by a light iron fence …' In *Cours de Peintures par Principes*, which was written in 1708 and translated into English in 1743 as *The Principles of Painting*, Roger de Piles expresses something of the unique visual character 'Of Verdure, or Turfing' in the garden: '… the greenness with which the herbs colour the ground … is done several ways; and the diversity proceeds not only from the nature of the plants, which, for the most part, have their particular verdures, but also from the change of seasons, and the colour of the earth, when the herbs are but thin sown. By this variety, a painter may chuse or unite, in the same tract of land, several sorts of greens intermixed and blended together … because this diversity of greens, as it is often found in nature, gives a character of truth to those parts, where it is properly used.'

The medieval Albertus Magnus describes one of the lawn's functions, writing: 'Pleasure gardens … are in fact mainly designed for the delight of two senses, viz sight and smell. They are therefore provided rather by

Fresh air and fun! TOP *The little girls of* c. *1915 look ready to create crazy croquet.*
BOTTOM *How could the gardener at the Limes* c. *1905 even consider asking who's for tennis?*

removing what especially requires cultivation: for the sight is in no way so pleasantly refreshed as by fine and close grass kept short.' Francis Bacon echoes this sentiment in his 1621 essay 'On Gardens' with his assertion that 'nothing is more pleasant to the eye than green grass kept finely shorn'.

Though he advised cottagers not to waste precious land with unproductive lawns, in *Cottage Economy* (1823) William Cobbett recommends lawns for larger Regency gardens for, he says, 'grass is another great ornament, and, perhaps, if kept in neat order, the greatest of all'.

However, not everyone likes lawns. In China lawns do not feature in traditional gardens and a Chinese visitor to England in the 1920s was said to have described 'a mown and bordered lawn' as something 'which, while no doubt of interest to a cow, offers nothing to the intellect of a human being'.

SCYTHING AND MOWING

Writing seven years before the invention of the lawnmower, J.B. Papworth takes a swipe at the scyther: 'The lawn is in general very much restricted in point of size, from the labor that is imagined necessary to keep it mown: but this is a great error – perhaps proceeding from the silly habit that the mower has of indicating his industry by the frequent use of the grit stone in sharpening his scythe: and generally at the time of the morning when such noises are most tormenting.' Henry A. Bright, on the other hand, in *A Year in a Lancashire Garden* (1901) rejoices in the sound of the scythe: 'But there are sounds that haunt a garden hardly less delightful than its sights and scents. What sound has more poetry in it than when in the early morning one hears the strong sharp sweep of the scythe, as it whistles through the falling grass, or the shrill murmur of the blade upon the whetstone; and, in spite of mowing machines, at times one hears the old sound still.'

Despite the invention of the lawnmower in 1830, many with small gardens continued to use scythes or sickles. The scythe still reigned supreme in 1842 when Andrew Downing wrote *Cottage Residences*. He notes: 'Frequent mowing is necessary to insure that velvet-like appearance so much admired in English lawns. To perform this operation neatly, the mower must be provided with a scythe the blade of which is very broad, and hung nearly parallel to the surface of the lawn.' Scythes were individually adapted to match the mower's height. And scything, according to Robert Thompson, head gardener to the Royal Horticultural Society in 1859, required some skill. He observes that 'nothing but a considerable

amount of practice will make a man a good mower of lawns'. The strimmer is the scythe's modern replacement.

The lawnmower, however, has many advantages. Its inventor, Edwin Budding, described its virtues when he patented it in 1830: '... grass growing in the shade and too weak to stand against the scythe may be cut by this machine as closely as required, and the eye will never be offended by those circular sears, inequalities, and bare places so commonly made by the best mowers with the scythe, and which continue visible for several days.' Appealing to the better sort, he says: 'Country gentlemen may find, in using the machine themselves, an amusing, useful and healthy exercise.'

In 1862 Edward Kemp, exploring economy of labour and cost, saw the mower's cost effectiveness. In *The Gardener's Chronicle* he concludes: '... [the] lawn is, on the whole, less expensive to keep up than flower-beds and borders, and should therefore abound where economy of keeping is sought ... in comparison with the use of a scythe, the saving from the employment of a mowing-machine will be very considerable.'

The general population must have agreed with Kemp's sentiment that lawns were more economical because by 1939 it was calculated that lawns covered more than 75 per cent of England's total garden area. The argument continues today, when economy must be balanced against the quality of lawn you seek – green, bowling alley or springy sward?

ABOVE *This army of gardeners was made up of patients at Mount Vernon Hospital, Northwood, Middlesex, during the First World War.* RIGHT *Lawn-trimming machines for every need.*

WILLIAM COOPER, 755, Old Kent Road, London, S.E.
HORTICULTURAL   PROVIDER.

Double-Handed Lawn Mower.

No. 520.

To cut 16 inches ...   . Price £6   0   0
This can be worked by one man on an even lawn.
To cut 18 inches ...   . Price £6 10   0
By man and boy.
„   20 inches ...   .   „   7   0   0
By man and boy.
„   22 inches ...   .   „   8 10   0
By two men. If made stronger, suitable for Donkey, 30s. extra.
„   24 inches ...   . Price £9   0   0
If made stronger, suitable for Donkey, 30s. extra.
Prices of Packing Cases for 16in., 5s. ; 18in. and 20in., 6s. ; 22in. and 24in., 7s.
If returned, two-thirds will be allowed for them.

Lawn Edge Clipper.

This Machine supplies a long-felt want
for trimming off the grass blades which
spring from the edge of the sod and
overhang the walks and flower-beds.

PRICES.
No. 1 ... £1 5s. 6d. | No. 2 ... £1 14s.

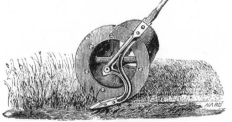

No. 521.

MAKING A LAWN

On the subject of making a lawn, William Cobbett makes the point that 'If grass be about to be laid down, the ground should be well prepared: if too poor to keep the grass fresh through a hot summer, it should be made richer, and always deeply moved.'

Likewise Albertus Magnus argues for good preparation:

It is impossible to produce [a good lawn] except with rich and firm soil; so it behoves the man who would prepare the site for a pleasure garden, first to clear it well from the roots of weeds, which can scarcely be done unless the roots are first dug out and the site levelled, and the whole well flooded with boiling water so that the fragments of roots and seeds remaining in the earth may not by any means sprout forth. Then the whole plot is to be covered with rich turf of flourishing grass, the turves beaten down with broad wood mallets and plants of grass trodden into the ground until they cannot be seen or scarcely anything of them perceived. For then little by little they may spring forth closely and cover the surface like a green cloth.

On the subject of beating, in *Grass: A new and thoroughly practical book on Grass for ornamental Lawns and all purposes of Sports and Games* (1924) – a title to inspire confidence – A.J. Macself says: 'In regard to the use of the beater discretion is necessary. It is quite in order, and, in fact, essential that the turf shall be made tolerably firm, but it is fallacious to suppose that turf can endure such thrashing with a beater that it is flattened out like a pancake as to abuse the legitimate purpose of the roller. Both these implements are sheer instruments of torture and wanton mischief in many hands.'

Richard Surflete in his 1616 translation of the *Maison Rustique* suggests a less severe method, saying that a lawn should be 'daunced upon with the feete, and the beater or pauing beetle lightly passing ouer them, in such sort as that within a short time after, the grass may begin to peepe up and put foorth like small haires; and finallie it is made the sporting greenplot for Ladies and Gentlewomen to recreate their spirits in.'

Treading is good for chamomile lawns, according to the old country saying 'Like a camomile bed, the more it is trodden, the more it will spread' – a saying that Shakespeare recalled in *Henry IV* when Falstaff observes: 'Though the Camomile the more it is trodden on the faster it grow, yet

youth the more it is wasted the sooner it wears.' Lawns of chamomile
(*Chamaemelum nobile*) have not only a pleasing verdancy but also a glorious
apple scent. In his section on flowers Albertus Magnus recommends
chamomile as being ideal for raised turf seats.

Francis Bacon recommends other scented plants that benefit from
treading in his essay 'On Gardens', a poetic voyage through Elizabethan and
early Jacobean gardens, which he wrote in the last years of his life. 'But
those which perfume the air most delightfully, not passed by as the rest but
being trodden upon and crushed, are three; that is, burnet, wild thyme, and
water mints. Therefore you are to set whole alleys of them, to have the
pleasure when you walk or tread.' Burnet (*Sanguisorba minor*) will give a
flowery mead effect; wild thyme (*Thymus serpyllum*) thrives in very dry, sunny
spots; and even better than water mint would be the diminutive Corsican
mint (*Mentha requenii*), whicih likes a shady, preferably damp spot.

For those laying their lawns with grass turf, Cobbett advises: 'To sow
grass is not the way to have fine grass plats; but to cut the turf from a
common or from some very ancient and closely-pressed pasture where the
herbage is fine. From our finest Downs, or from spots in our Commons,
the turf is generally taken; and, short grass, as the gardeners call it, is seen
in perfection, I believe, nowhere but in England.'

Similar tips were available for finding suitable turves, one saying that
'the best ... are had in the most hungry Common, and where the grass is
thick and short'. In 1702 when the Privy Garden at Hampton Court Palace
was created for William III, the local sheep-nibbled pastures of Molesey
Common were considered ideal as a source of turf for it. When the garden
was restored in 1994, turf found on Romsey Marsh in Kent was used, being
both sheep-nibbled and closest in character and appearance to that of the
early eighteenth-century original.

For those who want to produce a lawn from seed, Philip Miller lists
thirty-five varieties of 'Gramen' in his *Gardener's Dictionary* (1731) – grasses
for every site. He advocates: 'The best Season for sowing of Grass Seed is
the latter End of August, and Beginning of September, that the Grass may
be well rooted before the Frost sets in, which is apt to turn the plants out
of the Ground, when they are not well rooted. This Seed should be sown
in moist Weather, or when there is a Prospect of Showers, which will soon
bring the Grass up; for the Earth being at that Season warm, the Moisture
will cause the Seeds to vegetate in a few Days.' His advice holds good today,

provided that earlier in the season you have prepared a billiard-table-smooth area on which to sow. As Miller goes on to explain: 'The Land on which Grass-seed is intended to be sown, should be well ploughed and cleared from the Roots of noxious Weeds, such as Couch Grass, Fern, Rushes, Heath, Gorse, Broom, Rest-Harrow, etc. which if left in the Ground, will soon get the better of the Grass, and overrun the Land … it will be a good Method to plough up the Surface in April, and let it lie some time to dry, then lay it in small Heaps, and burn it. The Ashes so produced, when spread on the land, will be a good Manure for it.' Ashes will not only provide potash but the fire will cleanse and sterilize the soil, a system used by farmers off and on for millennia. Miller continues:

> Before the Seed is sown, the Surface of the Ground should be made level and fine, otherwise the Seed will be buried unequal … it must be gently harrowed in, and the Ground rolled with a wooden Roller; which will make the Surface even, and prevent the seeds being blown in

ABOVE *Beeton's* Shilling Gardener *carried advertisements for recommended garden products. It is good to know that canary guano 'May be used by a Lady'.*

Patches. When the Grass comes up, if there should be any bare Spots, … they may be sown again, and the Ground rolled, which will fix the Seeds; and the first kindly Showers will bring up the Grass, and make it very thick … The Following Spring, if there should be any Thistles, Ragwort, or such other troublesome Weeds, come up among the Grass, they shou'd be carefully cut up with a Spaddle before they grow large; and this should be repeated two or three times in the Summer.

A spaddle is a small spade, defined by William Caxton in 1474 as being 'for to delve and labour ther-with the erthe'.

MAINTENANCE

Thomas Tusser in his *Five Hundred Points of Good Husbandry* (1573) turns the gardener out in January to 'Rid grasse of bones, of sticks and stones', before the grass comes up and masks them.

The reader of Beeton's *Shilling Gardener* learnt:

During the spring, and the early summer months, all garden turf and lawns will require very great attention … (and we must remember that the general appearance of the whole garden depends much upon the state of the turf), it is at such times that the broom and roll must be kept in constant use. If the grass from the nature of the soil, is inclined to grow rank and coarse, it will be much improved by a good dressing of sand all over it; if, on the other hand it has a tendency to scald and burn up, it will receive great benefit from a sprinkling of good guano or soot just before a shower of rain.

In his *New Dictionary of Every-day Gardening* Beeton adds: 'if the lawn be not so near the house as to render such applications objectionable'. Today there are not only a range of lawn feeds available but also Green Waste, which can be applied inoffensively. Mr Macself, however, does not agree

with the need for sand: 'Will it not occur to the reader that it is needless extravagance to dress the whole lawn, grass as well as weeds, with lawn sand?' The *New Dictionary* also says:

A daisy rake. See page 199 to see how it is 'very easily made'.

Before regular mowing commences, it will be well to go over all grass, carefully removing rank and unsightly weeds, daisies, dandelions, the little buttercup etc., etc. Wherever the turf is mossy, it is a very good plan to rake it well with a sharp five-toothed rake; but it must be borne in mind that under-draining is the only effectual cure for moss. Daisies should never be allowed to flower; a good daisy rake, with a little trouble, will remove all flowers as they come out; but the only plan to clear a lawn effectually of these disagreeable weeds is to take them out with the daisy fork wherever they are found. Daisies, and all weeds, are more easily removed in wet weather, or after a shower than when the ground is dry. The tool may be used by any lady or child; and in process of time the most hopeless pieces of grass may be cleared by it. Turf, quite white with daisies in the spring, may be cleared entirely in the course of a season. The neat appearance of the garden will repay the time and trouble spent in the continual use of the daisy fork. A few showers of rain and a heavy roll will soon obliterate the holes that are made; and fine grass will not be long in filling up the spaces hitherto occupied by daisies and weeds.

There would be no possibility of children making daisy chains under this regime.

Lawn weeds vex and even obsess Victorian and twentieth-century writers. In a section called 'Hints on Laying down Lawns with Grass Seeds and the Improvement of Old Turf', Jane Loudon says: 'Annual weeds indigenous to the soil are almost sure to come up; these can easily be checked, if not destroyed, by mowing them off as soon as they make their appearance. Plantain, dandelions, and daisies must be cut up each one singly about an inch below the surface (not deeper) and a teaspoonful of salt dropped over the cut part.' Beeton could not abide dandelions in the lawn and also recommends the use of salt: 'Dandelions, to Kill Cut the tops off in the spring, and place a pinch of salt, or a little gas-tar, on the fresh wound.' When cutting off the tops, remove all the rosette so that the top of the tap root is exposed. Gas tar might be hard to locate.

Cobbett says that 'grass … ought to be as smooth as cloth. If thistles or dandelions, or even daisies, come amongst the grass, the mowing of them off is not enough, for each will make a circle round the crown of its root and will overpower the grass. This, however is easily cured by cutting these roots off deeply with a knife, and pulling them up. This done during two summers successively, will destroy the dandelions and the thistles; and, as to the daisies, which have a shallow root, they may easily be kept down, if not extirpated.'

PESTS
Myriad writers concern themselves with lawn pests. Macself discusses the problems of ants. 'Among many remedies or destroyers I have used one of the safest where grass is concerned is to saturate the nest with strong camphor-water.' In his *New Dictionary* Beeton suggests other methods:

> Ants, to Destroy Place an inverted garden-pot over the nest, and the ants will work into it. Remove the pot in a day or two by placing a spade underneath it; then plunge it, with its contents, into boiling water, and repeat the process if necessary. Ants may be expelled from any particular plant by sprinkling it well with sulphur; they may also be kept away from wall-fruit, and other fruit while ripening, by drawing a broad band with chalk along the wall near the ground, and round the stem of the trees.

For moles, which can induce apoplexy in the mildest of gardeners, Robert Sharrock's 1694 deterrent was: 'Take red herrings and, cutting them to pieces, burn the pieces on the molehills, or you may put garlicke or leeks in the mouths of their Hills' – and then go on holiday.

In *A General History of Quadrapeds* (1790) Thomas Bewick writes: 'The Mole is mostly found in grounds where the soil is loose and soft, and affords the greatest quantity of worms and insects, on which it feeds ... In the act of forming its tracks or runs, it throws up large heaps of mould, which are extremely troublesome and injurious in ... cultivated grounds. Its destruction is consequently an object of importance to ... gardeners.' He also notes: 'The ingenious Mr. Burn, hatter, of Newcastle upon Tyne, has lately discovered a method whereby the exquisitely fine fur of this noxious, and hitherto despised animal, is likely to become of the greatest importance and utility to the public: By incorporating it with other materials, it forms a stame of peculiar strength and beauty for the purpose of making hats, superior to any that has hitherto been made use of.' Later, Victorian children earned pennies by selling moleskins.

In *The Art of Gardening* (1677) Worlidge suggests arming yourself with a spaddle – the tool that Miller advised using for rooting out troublesome weeds in lawns – to exterminate troublesome moles: 'Others destroy them very expeditiously by a spaddle, waiting in the mornings when the usually stir.' When they saw the tunnel tremble, they whacked the casts with the spaddle, the shock of the reverberations apparently felling the mole.

In 'On Gardens', Francis Bacon suggests making a feature of the work of these black-velvet-jacketed gentlemen: 'I like also little Heaps, in the Nature of Mole-hils ... to be set, some with Wilde Thume; Some with Pincks; Some with Germander, that gives a good Flower to the Eye; Some with Periwinckle; Some with Violets; some with Strawberries; Some with Couslips; Some with Daisiers; Some with Red-Roses; Some with Lilium Convallium; Some with Sweet-Williams Red; Some with Beares-foot; And the like Low Flowers, being withal Sweet, and Sightly.' If the moles' tunnels are in use flowers planted on the 'little Heaps' will routinely lose their root systems, so you will need to plant them around the edges and then they can scramble up them.

'Daddy Longlegs, or Crane Fly', says the 1930s catalogue of Suttons & Sons of Reading, 'in its perfect form of a fly (Tipula oleracea) does no harm, but the grubs, known by the familiar name of 'leatherjackets' owing to the toughness of their skins, are terribly destructive.' By putting songbirds to good use Suttons appear to be early exponents of integrated pest control: 'Where song birds are scarce the Tipula is capable of utterly destroying grass ... but cultivation, aided by the robins, thrushes, nightingales, and other birds, will keep the insect within bounds, even after a hot summer favourable to its increase.' Which is a good excuse to have a bird table. However, today you can also buy nematodes that gorge on leatherjackets when watered on to the grass.

Hedges and boundaries

GARDEN VISITORS
'But Peter, who was very naughty, ran straight away to Mr. McGregor's garden, and squeezed under the gate! First he ate some lettuces and some French beans; and then he ate some radishes ...' Charming as Beatrix Potter made Peter Rabbit, rabbits are unwelcome guests in most gardens. Gertrude Jekyll gardened companionably with her cats but browsing Peter

Rabbits were out. She describes in *The Home Pussies* (1900) how she kept them out: 'Tabby, a fine whole-coloured silver tabby, frequents the nut-walk and pergola, and considers himself the warden of two gates, the hand hanging-gate through the Yew hedge and the five-barred gate that crosses the back road behind the summer-house. Both gates have wire-netting over their lower halves to prevent the passing of rabbits; indeed but for this necessity neither gate would be there.'

Many gardeners, however, especially urban ones, find cats a nuisance, and will therefore applaud *The Compleat Florist* of 1706: 'Dogs and Cats ought not to be suffer'd in a Flower Garden. Your Dogs, by their continual leaping, leave ugly Marks or Impressions upon the Surface of the Ground – and the Cats scattering their Ordure all about, then scraping the Earth to cover it, grub up many Plants.' Most gardeners would heartily endorse Sam Beeton, who writes in his *New Dictionary*: 'The efficient division of garden ground from that which surrounds it is a matter of the utmost importance, as it is necessary to protect it as much as possible from the incursion and raids of fowls and rabbits.'

Thomas Hill too argues for the need to protect a garden from intruders,

ABOVE   *Mrs Loudon allowed her fantasies full rein when illustrating 'Arch of Rock Work'. The full-size angel must have required confident fixing.*

observing in *The Gardener's Labyrinth* (1577): 'Forasmuch as the same may be thought a meere madness, to have chosen out a fit plot of ground, and to cast, digge, and dresse it seemly in all points; yet lying open day and night, as wel to the incursions and common haunt, as the injuries to be wrought and done by Robbers or Thieves, fowls and beast; for that cause I here mind to treat of sundry manners of fencing, and compassing in of the Garden grounds in ancient times.'

THORNY DEFENCES

To defend a property, today's gardener is unlikely to do as 'The Ancient Husbandmen' did who, as Hill described, quoting Columella and Varro, invented 'the casting up of banks and countermures of earth, round about the Garden plot, much like to the trenches in time of war about Bulwarks and Tents: and these they specially made neare to high waies or by Rivers, or Marshes, or Fens lying open, or other fields, that the Garden plot might on such wise be defended, from the damages and harmes both of Theeves, Cattel, and Land-floods.'

Likewise the belt-and-braces security that Cobbett advises in *The English Gardener* (1829) seems extreme:

> But ... if you can ... effectually protect the fortress against every species of attack. This protection is to be obtained by a hedge made of hawthorn, black thorn; or, still better, with honey locust, the thorns of the latter being just so many needles of about an inch and a half long ... stouter than a needle and less brittle ... Make a ditch six feet wide ... the bank ought to be hung very regularly with dead bushes ... the hedge, in addition to this ditch and bank, renders the storming literally impossible [to] besiegers of gardens.
>
> I make but one entrance into the garden ... This will be the weak part of the fortification. There must be a bridge over the ditch ... guarded on the top and on the sides by stout pieces of wood ... let the whole neighbourhood be convinced that forcible entry into the garden is not to be accomplished without infinite difficulty ... better than all the steel-traps, spring-guns and penal laws in the world.

But a hedge alone remains popular as a boundary. In the past thorny hedging plants such as hawthorn, berberis or *Rosa rugosa* were favoured by many, not least because they are visually more pleasing deterrents to intruders than other defences, such as broken glass on wall tops. (Glass used in this way, incidentally, is not just a modern phenomenon; there is an illustration that shows it along the top of a brick wall enclosing a northern French apothecary's garden in the fifteenth century.)

In 1372 when the Lord Bishop of Ely's *ortolani* or gardener presented his accounts for the bishop's London palace at present-day Holborn they included:

> Costs of the Vineyard and Curtilage and in divers labourers and women for digging the vines and curtilage, and also for cleansing and pulling up weeds in the curtilage, as appears by the parcels sewn to this account, 69s 1 d., and in thorns bought, viz. 4 cartloads of thorns for making the hedges round the great garden, 6s. 8d., and in the stipends of 2 men making 6 score and 1 perches of hedges round the same garden, 35s. 3 d., by the perch, 3 d. 111s. 1d ... In the wages of 1 boy digging in the vineyard, and in the curtilage from the last day of December until 17th day of April, in the feast of Easter, for 106 days, 17s. 8d., taking by the day, 2d.

Hill describes some suitable hedging plants and an ingenious method of planting them:

> The most commendable inclosure for every Garden plot, is a quick set hedge, made with brambles and white thorne: but the stronger and more defensive hedge is the same, which the singular Democritus in his Greek instructions of Husbandrie ... cunningly uttereth, and the same with ease and smal cost after this manner: Gather saith he, in a due season of the yeare, the seeds found in the red berries of the biggest and highest Briers ... the thorow ripe seeds of the brambles (running low by the ground) the ripe seeds of the white Thorne [hawthorn (*Cratageus* spp.)], and to these both the ripe Berries of the Goose-berry and Barberry trees: this done, mix and steepe for a time, all the Berries and seeds in the bending meale of Tares, unto the thickness of Honey: the same mixture lay diligently into old and untwisted Ship or Wel-ropes, or other long worne ropes, and fittered or broken into short pieces, being in a manner starke rotten, in such

order, that the seeds bestowed or couched within the soft haires of them, may be preserved and defended from the cold, unto the beginning of the spring. At which time where you minded that the inclosure or hedge shall runne and spring up, there digge in handsome manner, two smal furrows, and these either two or three foot asunder, and a mans foot and a halfe deep: into which lay your ropes with the seeds, covering them workmanly with light earth, and (if need shal require) water by sprinkling, or moisten the seeds, in the same wise again.

How delightfully evocative is 'starke rotten' as a description of a worn-out bit of rope! This tip is a good way of getting a naturalistic and impenetrable hedge of mixed species, with the advantage that you can lay your seed-enriched rope in as curved or geometric pattern as you wish. Make sure you have prepared a good trench. What joy to await the germination of the seeds and subsequent growth into a thorny tapestry hedge!

ORNAMENTAL EFFECTS

As Victorian tastes became more sophisticated, thorny hedges became less popular. Sam Beeton unenthusiastically writes in his *New Dictionary*: 'The different kinds of thorn certainly embrace all the constituents of a good hedge: they are of easy culture, quick growth, and capable of being trained in any direction; they branch out and thicken under pruning, and are not over particular as to soil; but there are many other plants far more ornamental which will fulfil all these conditions equally well.'

Hedging provides not only ornament in the garden, especially when clipped or topiarized, but formal structure. Reginald Blomfield, who trained as an architect, famously coined the word 'formal' to describe the balance of architecture with garden structure, in which hedges play a part – as he describes in *The Formal Garden in England* (1892):

Architects are often abused for ignoring the surroundings of their buildings in towns; ... if the reproach has force ... it applies with greater justice to those who control both the house and its surroundings, and yet deliberately set the two at variance. The object of formal gardening is to bring the two into harmony, to make the house grow out of its surrounds, and to prevent its being an excrescence on the face of nature ... The building cannot resemble anything in nature, unless you are content with a mud-hut and cover it with grass ... on the other hand, you can lay out the grounds, and later the levels, and plant hedges and trees exactly as you please; in a word, you can so control and modify the grounds as to bring nature into harmony with the house ... The harmony arrived at is not any trick of imitation, but an affair of a dominant idea which stamps its impress on house and grounds alike ... its trimmed hedges and alleys, its flower-beds bounded by the strong definite lines of box-edgings and the like – all will show the quality of order and restraint.

As ornament or boundaries, hedges have been made of various plants, not just thorny ones. In *Sylva, or a discourse on Forest trees* (1664) John Evelyn extols the beauty of a holly hedge: 'Is there under heaven a more glorious and refreshing object of the kind, than an impregnable Hedge of near three hundred foot in length, nine foot high and five in diameter, which I can shew in my poor gardens at any time of the year, glitt'ring with its arm'd and vernished leaves? the taller standards at orderly distances, blushing with their natural coral; It mocks at the rudest assaults of the weather, beasts of hedge breakers.' It was fortunate that John Evelyn did not have to worry about close neighbours at his magnificent garden at Sayes Court, in Deptford: otherwise in planting a hedge this size he might well have been the equivalent of today's unthinking planters of leylandii hedges. Hollies (*Ilex* spp.) offer a range of leaf shapes, heights and variegations, and, often shade tolerant, they make excellent hedges. Nibbling young holly shoots is an excellent tonic for pet rabbits if they are unwell.

Yew has been a popular hedging plant, but William Robinson, trained gardener and profligate writer, was no yew hedge enthusiast. In *The English Garden*, he writes: 'In old days, whether in a manor house or castle garden, the use of Yew hedges had some clear motive of shelter or division, ... or at a cottage door as a living shelter. But when we use Yew hedges from the mere desire for them, and without much thought of the ground ... we may find ourselves in trouble ... it being quite easy to secure ... support and shelter [with] walls, Oak palings, other trellises.' He also says, 'Yew is a danger, and a hedge of it should never be planted where animals come near.'

Blomfield too laments the use of yew or other conifer hedges, but for a different reason:

... the landscape gardener attempts to establish a sort of hierarchy of nature, based on much the same principle as that which distinguishes a gentleman by his incapacity to do any useful work. Directly it is proved that a plant or a tree is good for food, it is expelled from the flower garden without any regard to its intrinsic beauty. The hazel-hedge has gone, and the apple-tree ... Trained as an espalier it makes a beautiful hedge ... Yet the landscape gardener would shudder at the idea of planting a grove or hedge of apple trees in his garden. Instead of this he will give you a conifer or a monkey-puzzler ...

Instead of yew Robinson recommends 'Holly, Quick, or Cockspur Thorn, with a sprinkling of Sloe or Bullace here and there', adding 'Holly is the best evergreen.' He also says that 'Where shelter is much sought the hedge should not be clipped, and is much handsomer if free-grown.' Vita Sackville-West practised this philosophy at Sissinghurst to the extent that the yew rondel was reduced from an elegant circle to a belly button.

In choosing a hedging plant, gardeners would be well advised to follow Beeton's advice in his *New Dictionary of Every-day Gardening*: 'In forming any hedge ... The skill of the gardener is hardly anywhere more discernible than in the exercise of that statesmanlike quality which consists of putting the right thing in the right place.'

A SENSE OF ENCLOSURE

Apart from defence against intruders and ornament, hedges and other boundaries provide enclosure. Imprisoned at Windsor Castle from 1413 to 1424, James I of Scotland took solace from the enclosed view:

> Now there was made fast by the tower wall
> A garden fair, and in the corners set
> Was all the place, and hawthorn hedges knit
> That no one though he were near walking by
> Might there within scarce any one espy.
> So thick the branches and the leafage green
> Beshaded all the alleys that there were.

In his *Observations on Modern Gardening* of 1770 Thomas Whately describes a typical and attractive scene of 'a thick and lofty hedgerow, which

is enriched with woodbine, jessamine and every odoriferous plant'
surrounding a garden through which 'a path, generally of sand and gravel,
is conducted in a waving line and the turf on either hand is diversified with
little groups of shrubs, or firs, or of the smallest trees, and often with beds
of flowers ... in some parts ... carried between larger clumps of
evergreens, thickets of deciduous shrubs or still more considerable open
plantations ... and in every corner or vacant space is a rosary, a close or
open clump or a bed of flowers.'

The financial success of Alexander Pope's translation of Homer's *Iliad*
enabled the poet and gardener to buy in 1719 a villa on the river Thames at
Twickenham with 4 acres (1.6 hectares). He also translated Homer's *Odyssey*
(1725–6), which includes a description of the gardens of Alcinous, a direct
parallel with his own cherished gardens at Twickenham:

> Close to the Gates a spacious Garden lies,
> From Storms defended and inclement Skies:
> Four Acres was th'allotted Space of Ground,
> Fenc'd with a green Enclosure all around.
> Tall thriving Trees confest the fruitful Mold;
> The red'ning Apple ripens here to Gold.

Nothing tastes sweeter than warm fragrant berries straight off the bush. Are these fruit tasters
posing or surprised in guilt?

Cobbett recounts in *The English Gardener* the works of surely the most charitable garden encloser in history:

> Enclosing Under this head we are first to speak of the walls, which ought to be twelve feet high, two feet thick … The top, or coping, of the wall, ought to consist of semicircular bricks … the joints well grouted or cemented … wall trees cannot be placed on the outside, with any chance of utility, unless there be an effectual fence to protect the trees on that wall. I knew an old gentleman, one of whose garden walls … was unprotected except by a common hedge. Those persons of the village who were fond of wall-fruit, who had none of their own, and who were young enough to climb walls, used to leave him a very undue proportion of his fruit, and that not of the best quality … He therefore separated a strip … by a little fence, very convenient for getting over; turned this strip, which lay along against the wall, into kitchen garden ground … furnishing his juvenile neighbours with onions for their bread and cheese, as well as fruit for their dessert, ever after he kept the produce of the inside of the garden for himself.

Likewise the Impressionist artist Claude Monet kept the walls secure around his kitchen garden at the Maison Bleue but he halved the lower wall of his main house in Giverny so that passers-by could enjoy his flowers.

Enclosure also creates shelter, a quiet place to enjoy the garden in all the seasons. The Edwardian F.W. Burbidge describes the pleasures of a secluded garden in *The Book of the Scented Garden* (1905): 'Of course, all garths and gardens are enclosed, that is to say, fenced and more or less sheltered, but our 'garden enclosed' is meant to be a garden within a garden, a sort of 'holy of holies,' being at one and the same time a wind-sheltered sun-trap … As to the garden itself, its size and form may be anything provided that it is in keeping, or due proportion to its surroundings. In this particular instance it is to be a garden of sweet scented plants and flowers' – a description that has a ring of the sensuous lines in the Song of Solomon, 'My beloved is gone down into his garden, to the beds of spices, to feed in the gardens, and to gather lilies.'

A walled garden is an integral part of our garden history and used in literature to express many ideas including maidenhood or magical qualities as in Frances Hodgson Burnett's secret garden in her 1911 novel. Enclosure relates too to man's need to mark out his territory – expressed in the Bible in the Book of Deuteronomy: 'Cursed be he that removeth his neighbour's landmark. And all the people shall say Amen' (landmark here meaning boundary) – and for privacy.

Today the open-plan gardens of the 1960s and '70s are rapidly being lost as a result of a renewed desire for privacy not unlike that noted by Humphry Repton in 1816: 'It is now a melancholy truth, that every proprieter possess'd of land near a high road begins his improvements by excluding the world.'

Although it is said that 'A hedge between keeps friendship green', Marion Cran too saw the negative side of the desire for privacy when she observed the hedges of suburban gardens. In *Garden Wisdom* she writes:

Of Privacy and Privet There are few things so abused in this flower-loving land of ours as hedges. In the passion for privacy which seems to be an ingrained quality of our race, every strip of land between one house and the next is divided and surrounded by hedges of privet, laurel, hawthorn, box, or yew – mostly privet and laurel, I regret to say. And these greedy root-grabbers grow widely till whole miles of our suburban streets are a depressing vista of clipped hedges – nothing else; nothing light and graceful and fragrant ... Many a time I have spied a suburban householder out with his clippers in the balmy air of young summer, performing the toilet of his hedge surround – clipping, paring, almost polishing it. And I have felt sad to realise how many city workers try to satisfy a deep craving for garden work on this unprofitable and monotonous job ... in one of the new roads growing out North London way ... all looked like a Noah's ark road, so tidy, bright, and small; the little gay houses, the small glossy hedges about two and a half feet high dividing each tiny kingdom from the next ... I am a garden artist and look without pleasure – I know the menace of those grim babies.

When Cran started writing in 1910 suburban housing estates were built at a density of eight dwellings per acre; by the time she ceased in 1941 there were twelve to the acre.

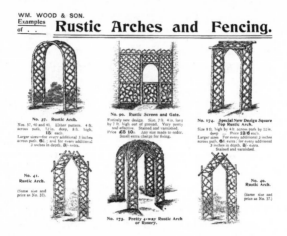

ABOVE *Ready-made options for the Victorian gardener who was not good at DIY.*
BELOW *John Worlidge shows a special picket fence by a garden of 'humane pleasures'.*

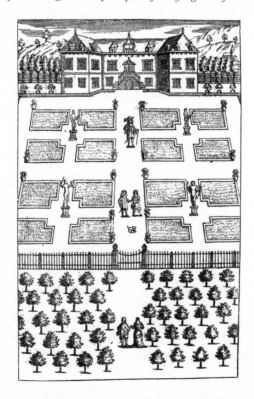

FENCING

Here is a selection of opinion in several hundred years of fencing choice – wood or iron, ornate or practical.

Humphry Repton says in 1816: 'The most effective fence against man is a park pale of 5 or 6 feet not placed perpendicularly but leaning a little outwards, the top over-hanging the foot about 10 inches – this is almost insurmountable by the most expert climber.'

John Worlidge writing in *The Art of Gardening* in 1677 suggests a complex wooden pattern: 'Use palings fixed along the edges with top cut into two: the middle vacancy being about one third part of the whole breadth, the two extream parts ... being cut with square pyramidal points ... As you stand against them they appear open and everything very conspicuous through them ... but as you view them obliquely they appear ful, only their sharp heads open and not unpleasant.'

Guaranteed to sound off, William Robinson says in *The English Flower Garden*: 'Where an open fence is wanted, nothing is so fine in form and colour as a split Oak fence and rails made of heart of Oak with stout posts. A sawn wood fence is not so good.' In fact it is only not so good if you are looking for a fence to last decades; as an interim and cheaper measure it is worth considering.

From the seventeenth century, iron fences became increasingly ornate in the hands of skilled craftsmen, Jean Tijou's repoussé screens at Hampton Court Palace being an exquisite survival. Their see-through nature meant that in the opening years of the eighteenth century William III was able to enjoy the view of the sun glinting on the Thames through them from his Privy Apartment.

The *Gentleman's Magazine* warned in 1769: 'You think yourselves very retired at home, and in perfect security by a barrier of iron rails, not considering that the hundred openings of this inclosure deprive you of that security, and that you have a hundred gates displayed, which leave a free communication from without, and expose you to plunder.'

But Hibberd recommends them to his readers in 1856: '... there is a large variety of fences in cast and wrought iron, in tasteful patterns suited for forming boundaries where views are to be preserved. There are many makers of such scattered up and down the country.' Sadly many iron fences were donated during the Second World War for recycling as armaments and in the end never used.

Robinson, no doubt, would have been pleased, for he says vehemently: 'The iron fence destroys the beauty of half the country seats in England, and the evil is growing every day. There are various serious objections to iron fencing, but we will only deal here with its effect on the landscape. Any picture is out of the question with an iron fence in the foreground.'

Perhaps he should have read 'The Cit's Country Box' in the *Connoisseur* magazine, published on 26 August 1756, with its sarcastic dig at the fashionable desire to have all things 'chinois':

> I cannot bear those nasty rails,
> Those ugly, broken, mouldy pales;
> Suppose, my dear, instead of these,
> We build a railing all Chinese.
> Although one hates to be exposed
> 'Tis dismal thus to be enclosed,
> I wish you'd fell those odious trees.
> Objects continual passing by
> Were something to amuse the eye,
> But to be pent within the walls –
> One might as well be at St. Paul's.

INVISIBLE BOUNDARIES

Robinson was enthusiastic about another kind of boundary, writing: 'Sunk fences of stone or brick are often of the highest value in the pleasure ground … as they help us to avoid the hideous mechanical fences of our day, and are often the best way of keeping open views, especially if planted with a garland of creeping plants.' Such boundaries are better known as ha-has, the name deriving from the exclamation people uttered either when they inadvertently fell down several feet into them or when they stopped on the brink in delight and surprise.

Ha-has, associated with large eighteenth-century landscapes, have the advantage of enabling the garden to 'borrow' the landscape. However, in *Rustic Adornments for Homes of Taste* (1856) Shirley Hibberd views them as neither decent nor tasteful:

> I must impress upon every … possessor of a garden surrounded by open country, the necessity of setting up a visible boundary line of a

substantial and definite character, and to all sunk fences, ditches, and invisible frontiers, let the reply be a derisive 'ha! ha!' ... for a boundary to a garden it is the last scheme that a man of taste will resort to. Why? well, just imagine a couple of ladies to be rambling in a lovely garden, and suddenly, as they emerge from ... a flowery lawn, they see half-a-dozen oxen staring them in the face, from what appears to be one of the lawns of the garden. They would scream and fly, and when assured there was a ha! ha! or, in other words, a ditch between the paddock and the garden they would still 'refuse to be comforted', and would not make another tour of the grounds unless each had her lover's arm to support and protect her.

If we are made secure against real or imagined dangers, it does not follow that a frantic horse, or a bellowing bull should form part of the apparent stock of a garden, and hence, if they must be shut out let the fence be visible ... in appearance, as well as in reality ...

Ornament

Ornament is an interesting adjunct to the flower garden. In 1899 Harold Peto, who designed luxuriant Italianate gardens for wealthy clients such as Daisy, Countess of Warwick at Easton Lodge, bought Iford Manor, where he lived until his death, using the house and gardens to display his eclectic collections of masonry and statuary. He also wrote an undated manuscript on the house and village called *The Boke of Iford*, in which he sums up his style: '... old buildings or fragments of masonry carry one's mind back to the past in a way that a garden of flowers only cannot do. Gardens that are too stony are equally unsatisfactory; it is the combination of the two in just proportion which is the most satisfactory.'

Shirley Hibberd looks for a rich display. Writing in *Rustic Adornments for Homes of Taste* (1856), he says 'A poverty of ornament is as miserable as an excess is ostentatious' and, describing a very princely mansion on the summit of a wooded hill:

The view from this frontage is magnificent ... but I do wonder that in front of such a breadth of brick-work and windows, in front of such a doorway too, there should be a pair of vases just large enough for the doorway of a tollhouse; compared with the house they are meant to

Instructions for the Ordering
AND Erection of Sun Dials.

"IONA."

Complete with Porcelain Dial
Equation Table, Bronzed
Metal Gnomon. Height of
Pedestal 3 ft.

Price **£3   7s.   6d.**

"FLORA."

Complete with Porcelain Dial
Equation Table, Bronzed
Metal Gnomon. Height of
Pedestal 3 ft.

Price **£3   12s.   6d.**

TO ORDER DIALS.

THE following details must be given when ordering Dials.

HORIZONTAL and EQUATORIAL. The latitude of the place of erection as shown on a map—thus, London, 51¼° N.; Philadelphia, 40° N.; Durban, 30° S.

VERTICAL. The latitude of the place of erection as above, also the aspect of the wall against which it is to be fixed. This can usually be found exactly from a plan of the house, &c., but if one is not available, place a box compass against the wall and note the magnetic aspect, then allow for the magnetic variation to find the true aspect. The magnetic variation cannot be given here as it differs, not only all over the world, but is also constantly changing.

TO ERECT DIALS.

VERTICAL. Bolt to the wall so that the sides and face are perfectly vertical as shown by a plumb line.

HORIZONTAL and EQUATORIAL. This is best done by the Sun, with the use of a good watch and a level. If an equatorial dial, first see that the pointer is against the correct latitude graduation on the arc. Note that the top of the pedestal is perfectly level and fill the recess with mixed Portland cement. Place the dial in position and revolve it till it shows the local solar time. Test it again for level and leave it for the cement to set. The best time to set dials is about midday.

They may also be set with a box compass. Proceed as above, placing one side of the box compass against the gnomon, revolving the dial till the sloping face of the gnomon points due **S.** or **N.,** according as the place is **N.** or **S.** of the Equator and allowing of course for the magnetic variation of the place. This method is inconvenient of application with equatorial dials.

LOCAL SOLAR TIME. To set a watch to local solar time, first get the standard mean time of the country and set the watch 1 minute fast of this for every ¼ degree the place is East, or slow if West of the meridian of the standard time. Thus, Bristol being 2½° W. of Greenwich, local time is 10 minutes slow of Greenwich time, and Calcutta being 8° East of Madras, the local time is 32 minutes fast of Madras standard time. This is local mean time. Then refer to the table of the equation of time, given below and on most dials, and against the date will be found a number of minutes marked fast or slow. As the wording states, fast means that clock time (mean time) is fast of solar time, so set back the watch the number of minutes against the date if marked fast, or set forward if marked slow.—Thus on September 21st the clock is 7 minutes slow, so set the watch on 7 minutes. The result is that the watch is giving local solar time.

embellish, they appear as if dropped there by accident by some wandering Italian … each vase has in it one small Tom Thumb geranium … a tree stump just as large as the two vases would be if they were melted into one. This decorated with one verbena, one geranium and a central handful of mignonette. Could anything be more miserable, more poverty struck, than such things in front of a mansion whence an earl might issue?

Impressionist gardeners Gertrude Jekyll and Claude Monet favoured pergolas and frames to sculpture. My personal favourites are display statues and sculptures on the grand scale: at the eighteenth-century Kentian landscape at Rousham in Oxfordshire and Geoffrey Jellicoe's inspired choices for Sutton Place in Surrey.

Many a smaller garden, too, tucks humour and classical reference in the tiniest corners, as Henry Bright shows. Toying with the idea of statuary for his garden, in *A Year in a Lancashire Garden* (1901) he writes:

Among my ideas – I cannot call it plans … I half fancy putting up a statue of some sort in a nook in the little wood, where the Beeches

ABOVE *For an extra five shillings you could buy 'Flora' to grace your garden.*

grow the tallest and the Elders are thickest. Such things were once common, and then they got so common, and often so out of place, that they became absurd. Every villa garden had its statue and its rockery.

Batty Langley has an amusing chapter about statues. He says – 'Nothing adds so much to the beauty and grandeur of gardens as fine statues, and nothing is more disagreeable than when they are wrongly placed; as Neptune on a terrace walk, mound, etc.; or Pan, the god of sheep, in a large basin, canal, or fountain;' and then, 'to prevent such absurdities,' he gives the most elaborate directions. Mars and Jupiter, Fame and Venus, Muses and Fates, Atlas, Hercules, and many more, are for open centres or lawns. Sylvanus, Actaeon, and Echo, are among those recommended for woods. Neptune, Oceanus, and the Naiades, will do for canals and fish-ponds. Pomona and the Hesperides for orchards, Flora and Runcina ('the goddess of weeding') for flower gardens, Bacchus for vineyards, Aeolus for high terrace walks ... I hope he would approve of my own very humble idea, which is a statue of Hyacinthus, – for, where I thought of placing it, the wild Hyacinthus or Bluebells will come clustering up, and make the grass all blue.

For a smaller garden, try to think creatively. Taking inspiration from Henry Bright, you could use hyacinths or bluebells to create spring 'water' features, planted in a flowing 'stream' under trees or shrubs. Or you could risk a Neptune or Naiade, or Oceanus' granddaughters, the Nereids. If you like to sip wine in the garden, introduce Bacchus, aka Dionysus, who represents not only the intoxicating effect of wine but its social and beneficial qualities which promote civilization and peace.

Toil

Soil

RECOGNITION OF GOOD SOIL

The Seventeenth Book of Pliny's *Historia Naturalis* opens with 'How to tell Good Soil'. Seeing is not enough, according to Pliny: it is the smell and taste of soil that will tell you if it is good.

> Well, to speak at a word, surely that ground is best of all other, which hath an aromatic smell and taste with it. Now if we list moreover to be better instructed, what kind of savour and odour that should be, which we would so gladly find in the earth; we may oftentimes meet with that scent, even when she is not stirred with the plough, but lieth still and quiet, namely, a little before the sun-setting, especially where a rainbow seemeth to settle and pitch her tips in the horizon: also, when after some long and continual drought, it beginneth to rain; for then being wet and drenched therewith, the earth will send up a vapour and exhalation (conceived from the sun) so heavenly and divine, as no perfume (how pleasant soever it be) is comparable to it. This smell there must be in it … which if a man find once, he may be assured it is a right good ground; for this rule never faileth.

In *De Re Rustica c.* AD 60–5, Lucius Junius Moderatus Columella advises touching the soil. If, he says, it 'sticks to the finger of the person holding it, in the manner of pitch, it is fertile'. Hill suggests in *The Gardener's Labryinth* (1577):

> … the Gardener by taking up a clod of earth, should esely trie the goodness of it after this manner: in considering whether the earth be neither hot and bare, not leane by sand, lacking a mixture of perfect earth: nor barren gravel, nor of the glistering pouder or dust of a leane stony ground, not the earth continual moist; for all these be the special defaults of a good and perfect earth. The best ground for a Garden, is the same judged to be, which in the Summer time is neither very drie, nor clayie, nor sandy and rough, nor endamaged with gapings, procured by heat of the Summer.

... The Gardener minding to trie and know a fat earth, for the use of a Garden, shall worke after this manner: in taking a little clod of the earth, and the same to sprinckle with fair water, kneading it well in the hand: which after appearing clammie, and cleaving or sticking to the fingers, doth undoubtedly witnesse that earth to have a fatnesse in it ... The Garden ground doth also require a sweetness to consist in it, which the Gardener shall easily find and know by taste of it: if so be he take up a clod of the earth in any part of the ground which most misliketh him, and moistning the clod with faire water in an earthern potsheard, doth after the dipping of the finger in this moist earth and water, let a drop softly fall on the tongue, he shall incontinent feele and perceive (by reason of the taste) of what condition the same is.

The Saturday gardening column in *The Times* of 16 March 1907 explains the relevance of soil texture to plants:

The problems of gardening in heavy soils are naturally quite different from those of gardening in light soils; for whereas the chief enemy of plants in light soils is drought and heat in summer, their chief enemy in heavy soils is damp and cold in winter. Climate is not the only condition which affects the hardiness of plants; soil has also to be considered; and many plants that are hardy on a light sandy soil are not hardy on a stiff clay, although the climate may be no colder ... drainage is the chief essential to success in a stiff soil: and it is necessary not merely to protect the plants from damp and cold, but also to make the ground fertile, for if the upper layer of the soil is charged with water, air cannot get into it, and without air those processes of decomposition which make soil fertile are impossible.

This advice applies particularly to Mediterranean plants and those on the edge of their zone of hardiness. The writer continues:

Speaking generally ... deep-rooting plants are most suitable to light soils, in which their roots protect them from drought, while shallow-rooting plants do best in heavy soils, where there is usually enough moisture on the surface even in summer to keep their roots cool. But this is only a general rule. Some deep-rooting plants, such as paeonies,

are never so fine as in a stiff soil, and many shallow-rooting plants will
not endure the cold and damp of a stiff clay … But some people find
the most difficult games the most interesting, and the born gardener
reveals his genius most when he has to deal with stiff clay or pure sand.

SOIL IMPROVEMENT

As we fill ever more land sites with rubbish, we would do well to consider
carefully what we can recycle and use to improve soil, taking inspiration
from historical advice on muck – comical and probably hazardous to health
as some of it is.

Pliny provides a historical perspective on the subject of dung before
launching into its delights:

The first that devised mucking of grounds, was … Augeas, a king in
Greece … Varro esteemeth the dung of blackbirds … above all others
… In the second degreeth of goodness Columella rangeth pigeons'
dung … third place he giveth to that of hens, and other land pullen,
rejecting altogether the dung of waterfowl … Next unto the ordure

By the late nineteenth century recycling waste was losing the battle against the rise of artificial fertilizers.

and urine of man's body, the filthy dung of swine ... that of goats; ... of sheep, then of kine and oxen; and lastly of cart-jades, mules, asses, and such like ... riddle and sift their dung ... through sieves .... turneth it into a pleasant smell, and looketh lovely withal.

Columella himself says:

> ... the gardener
> Should with rich mould or asses' solid dung
> Or other ordure glut the starving earth
> Bearing full baskets straining with the weight,
> Nor should he hesitate to bring as food
> For new-ploughed fallow-ground whatever stuff
> The privy vomits from its filthy sewers.

Like many of the manures this and other writers recommend, some of Beeton's recommendations in his *Shilling Gardening Book* are either no longer produced or now available in more acceptable forms. 'We hear and read a

ABOVE *Engulfed by ash-laden air, they womanfully riddle the bonfire debris.*

great deal of all manner of exciting composts, such as guano, night-soil, bullock's blood, offal of the slaughterhouse, sugar-bakers' scum, and various other not very nice material; but all this resolves itself in the single fact that all animal matter, as well as animal dung, enriches the ground - bone-dust, shavings of horn and hoofs among the rest. ... Horse dung varies in its composition according to the food of the animal; it is most valuable when they are fed upon grain, being then firm in consistence and rich in phosphates.' Today commercial organic growers have difficulties sourcing manure from animals on organic diets.

Cobbett's advice from *The English Gardener* reminds me of how children used to be sent out to gather up horse droppings off the road for their parents' gardens. 'If you have not enough of dung from the stable-door, some from cow-stalls, sheep-yards, and even long stuff from pig-beds or pig-styes, half-stained litter; or anything of a grassy kind, and not entirely dry, will lend you assistance; but, let it be understood, that the best of all possible materials ... is dung from the stables of corn-fed horses; and the next best comes from a sheep-yard or from stalls where ewes and sucking lambs have been kept.'

Gertrude Jekyll too expressed the value of horse dung in her essay 'Gardening for Short Tenancies', published in 1900. 'But official dwellers in and about the camp [at Aldershot] have one grand advantage ... in a vast supply of stable manure. And though it has neither the cooling quality of cow manure nor the richness of pig, yet anything of a nourishing nature in so poor a soil is of extreme value, especially as it also puts into the ground the precious chemical constituents of the decayed straw.' It is worth remembering that raw manure should not be in direct contact with roots, stems or leaves.

The Reverend Henry Burgess appreciated that gardeners might be reluctant to handle dung. In *The Amateur Gardener's Year-Book* (1854) he writes:

I know ladies who love gardening, and have a limited number of favourites which they tend with their own fair hands, but are often at fault in reference to the soil which they should employ for potting ... Night soil and pigeons-dung and sugar baker's scum are rather ill-favoured materials to have to manipulate ... Good turfy loam from an old meadow is the ne plus ultra ... its value cannot be too highly estimated. Get as much of the turf with it as you can, and put it in a heap for twelve months … The other material is thoroughly-rotted stable dung … Two years a requisite to produce this complete rottenness. In the autumn these materials should be well mixed in equal quantities, and turned over two or three times in the winter.

Both Loudons exhorted their readers to wear gardening gloves when dealing with dung, which would seem essential.

Another kind of animal dung appears in a spectacular Victorian recipe for a potting compost: '2 barrows full of goose dung, steeped in blood; 2 of sugar-baker's scum; 2 of night soil; and 2 of fine yellow loam. Prepare and turn and mix monthly for 2 years.' It was recommended for auriculas, which were popular in Victorian times, when gardeners created auricula theatres for a spring display.

Night soil is a splendid euphemism, recalling the historic nightly collections from urban cesspools and privies, by comparison with the more prosaic Victorian saying 'No turd, no gardener'. Both reflect the fact that human excrement is a valuable soil improver. Sewage plants today process their waste for farmers and gardeners, while we have a septic tank in the garden whose finger drains have nurtured our orchard for nearly thirty years.

Three examples of potent garden fertilizers.

Thompson's *Gardener's Assistant* takes a scientific stance on the subject:

Analysis shows that fresh human excrements are richer in fertilizing matters than those of farm animals. The food of man is usually much more concentrated than that of animals. It is richer in respect of nitrogen and phosphates, consequently the excrements derived from such food are correspondingly concentrated and valuable for the growth of plants.

Ordinary night-soil does not contain so large a proportion of fertilizing matters as fresh excrement, being mixed with water, ashes, soil, and other rubbish. It should be deodorized before it is employed in the garden by mixing it with charcoal dust, gypsum, dry earth, sifted ashes, and quicklime.

Night-soil forms an excellent manure for Turnips, the Cabbage tribe, and Celery, and indeed for many other crops, though it is not so much employed as it deserves to be, perhaps on account of its being erroneously supposed to affect the flavour of the plants.

OTHER KINDS OF SOIL IMPROVERS

Muck, of course, is not the only kind of soil improver. The Reverend Timothy Dwight, who in *Travels in New York and New England (1821–22)* described Manhattan Island in 1791 as having 'cheerful habitations, with well stocked gardens, and neat enclosures', was particularly impressed by the recycling efforts of the New York market gardeners:

... the inhabitants, with a laudable spirit of enterprise, have set themselves to collect manure, wherever it could be obtained. Not content with what they could make, and find, on their own farms, and shores, they have sent their vessels up the Hudson, and loaded them with the residuum of potash manufactories; gleaned the streets of New York; and have imported various kinds of manure from New-Haven; have swept the sound; and covered their fields with the immense shoals of whitefish with which in the beginning of summer its waters are replenished. No manure is so cheap as this, where the fish abound: none is so rich: and few are so lasting.

Another report of about 1800 describes this practice: 'A single net has taken 200,000 in a day ... These fish are sometimes laid in furrows, and voered with the plough. Sometimes they are laid singly on the hills of maize, and covered with the hoe. At other times they are collected in heaps, formed with other materials into a compost; carted upon the ground; and spread in the same manner, as manure from the stable ... They are sold for a dollar a thousand; and are said to affect the soil advantageously for a considerable length of time.'

If you are composting fish remains, bury them at least a spit deep, and do not put them on the compost heap, as not only will the smell be antisocial but also the heap will be likely to attract rats, foxes and any neighbourhood cats. It is easier to use dried fish products and seaweed, which is also a good soil improver, both of which we are lucky enough to be able to buy now.

After twenty years of careful experimentation with soils and manures, Thomas Rivers perfected his recipe for ensuring good soil. He writes: 'The most suitable soil is good turfy loam not too heavy; to five barrow-loads of this, add one of sifted old mortar rubbish or road scrapings with plenty of grit in it, one bushel of wood ashes and one peck of half-inch bones.' The latter provide potash and phosphates to ripen wood and fruits.

In William Robinson's revised version of Jane Loudon's *The Amateur Gardener* (1880) there is a small section dedicated to 'Wood Ashes and their Uses', in which I detect more of the revisor than the originator. Robinson was obsessively against the use of coal and insisted that both heating and cooking stoves at Gravetye burnt only wood. Perhaps, then, rather than 'she' it might be more correct to say 'they' write:

During the past year we have had ample means of testing the value of wood ashes or charred earth, both as a means of warding off the attacks of slugs and other garden pests from tender vegetables, and as a means of enriching growth ... We find them to be the best and safest of manures for mixing with new vine borders, also with the potting soil for many exotic plants. If many of the so-called artificial manures were composed exclusively of pure wood ashes, purchasers would have less cause to complain than they frequently now have; for, in the open quarters devoted to vegetable culture, the spots on which rubbish heaps have been burned are always indicated by the luxuriance of succeeding crops.

Perhaps not surprisingly, Pliny's compatriots were not always happy with the use of dung. Thomas Hill describes how

> There were in ancient time, as Pliny recordeth, certaine wittie Husbandmen, that wholly refused and forbad the dunging of Gardens placed nigh to the dwelling houses: in that this dunging might not onely infect the aire thereabout, but cause also the crescent rings to prove both unsavorier and more corrupt. And in this matter the worthy writers of Husbandry commended highly the Greek Poet Hesiodus, which writing very cunningly of Husbandry, omitted the dunging of the fields, and Gardens plots, contented rather to counsell unto healthfulnesse, then willed the same to fertility. Insomuch as it was supposed enough at that time, to have fatned the fields and Garden plots, with the leaves and empty cods of the Beanes, peason, Tares, and such like, turned work-manly in with the earth in due season of the yeare, and not to have employed or dunged the ground with a rotten and pestilent matter, incommodious to man and the Plants.

Peas and beans fix nitrogen in the soil by means of nodules in their roots, and their haulms when turned into the soil add valuable humus without odour.

Cobbett, too, argues for the use of other sorts of manures apart from dung.

> I have now to speak on the subject of manures as adapted to a garden. Different plants require different sorts of manure and different quantities. It is certainly true that dung is not the best sort of manure for a garden: it may be mixed with other matter, and, if very well rotted, and almost in an earthy state, it may not be amiss; but if otherwise used it certainly makes the garden vegetables coarse and gross compared to what they are when raised with the aid of ashes, lime, chaff, rags, salt, and composts. Besides, dung creates innumerable weeds … A great deal more is done by the fermentation of manures than people generally imagine: the shovellings of grass and turf from the sides of roads; weeds or roots of weeds raked off from a field; these laid in a great heap and turned frequently during the year, having ashes (of wood), lime, rags, salt in a small proportion, mixed with the

rest of the heap, make excellent manure. Provision of manure like this ought to be made, one heap being always ready to succeed another.

Today careful inclusion of lawn clippings in a compost heap can act as a substitute for some of these.

APPLICATION

How much manure do plants require? George Mount, who contributed 'Culture of Roses' in *Garden Colour* (1905), says of roses: 'A good moderately stiff loam is the best soil, but any soil will grow them if properly prepared. The soil should be double dug (not trenched) to a depth of 18 inches, and if it is very light or sandy, it is improved by an addition of heavy clay or loam. If too stiff, some light, well-rotted manure, and rough sharp sand, etc., is an improvement. Some well-rotted manure may also be dug in before planting.' If you do this, make sure that none of it touches the rose's roots as even well-rotted manure can burn them.

Robinson had other ideas. In *The English Flower Garden* (1883), he writes: 'In past years an enormous amount of manure was used in gardens in excess of what the plants really needed. Deep soil and a good free texture soil is quite as important. Let us not forget that some so-called artificial

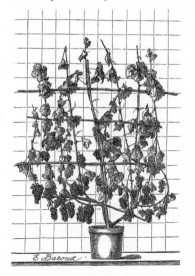
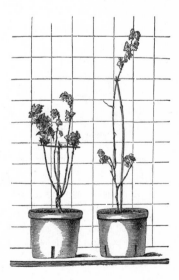

Spot the vine that has had regular dressings of manure.

manures are really natural, such as bone and other fertilisers, which may be used when helpful; but in my garden, where we have certainly the finest Roses, for many years we use no stable manure.'

Certainly not all plants benefit from manure. The Gospel of St Luke describes how 'A certain man had a fig tree planted in his vineyard; and he came and sought fruit thereon, and found none. Then said he unto the dresser of his vineyard, Behold, these three years I come seeking fruit on this fig tree, and find none: cut it down; why cumbereth it the ground? And he answering said unto him, Lord, let it alone this year also, till I shall dig about it, and dung it: And if it bear fruit, well: and if not, then after that thou shalt cut it down.' The fig tree was condemned! Manuring figs encourages luscious leaf growth not fruit. A lime dressing every third year and root restriction are more likely to lead to fruit bearing.

On the subject of figs, Gerard makes an interesting and visually pleasing suggestion in his *Herball* (1597): 'Garden rue joyeth in sunny and open places: it prospereth in rough and bricky ground and among ashes ... Pliny saith that there is such friendship between it and the fig-tree, that it prospers no where so well as under the fig tree.' I have done this successfully.

Digging

The pleasure of a Garden being thus demonstrated, I shall conclude with the profit thereof. First for household occasions, for there is not a day passeth over our heads but we have need of one thing or other that groweth within their circumference. We cannot make so much as a little good Pottage without Herbes, which give an admirable relish and make them wholesome for our Bodies. In a Garden there be Turnips and Carrots which serve for sauce, and if meat be wanting for that too. Neither doth it afford us Aliment only, but Physic ... But besides this inestimable profit, there is another not much inferior to it, and that is the wholesom exercise a man may use.

Dr. Pinck, later Ward of New College in Oxon, whereof I was once a Member ... was a very learned Man, and well versed in Physick,

ABOVE *Not only a guzzler of slugs but a delightful frontispiece to Hole's* Our Gardens (1899).

and truly he would rise very betimes in the morning, even in his later dayes, when he was almost fourscore years old, and going into his Garden, he would take a Mattock or Spade, digging there an houre or two, which he found very advantageous to his health. A Man worthy to be imitated, not only in this, but also in many other things, especially in his charitable Provisions for bringing up of poore Children.

And if Gentlemen which have little else to doe, would be ruled by me, I would advise them to spend their spare time in their Gardens; either in digging, setting, weeding, or the like, that which there is no better way in the world to preserve health. If a man want an Appetite to his Victuals, the smell of the Earth new turned up, by digging with a Spade will procure it, and if he be inclined to a Consumption it will recover him.

The man who extols such exercise was William Coles, under 'Joys of a Garden' in *The Art of Simpling* (1656). His contemporary Nicholas Culpeper also favoured 'Moderate exercise'. In *A Directory for Midwives* (1651) he writes:

... by opening the pores, [it] cleaneth the blood of thos fuliginous and sooty vapours which usually offend it; and this is the reason sweating is such a good remedy in feavours. Now then, if the blood be cleansed of what offends it, or corrupts it before it be sent down to the testicles to be conducted into seed, the children bred of this purified seed must needs be stronger and by consequence more subject to live. Moderate exercise of the parents conduceth much to the lives of the children.

Culpeper also believes in the benefit of fresh air:

The operation of air to the body of man, is as great as meat and drink. For it helpeth to engender the vital and animal spirit, which causeth in a man, apprehension, imagination, fancy, opinion, consent, judgement, reason, resolution, discerning, knowledge, remembrance, calling to mind, mirth, joy, hope, trust, humanity, boldness, mercy, fear, sadness, dispair, hatred, malice, mildness, stubbornness, and indeed though the bulk of the body be nourished by food, the air carries the greatest swing in all the actions thereof; for it's the causer of life, health, sickness, death to mortals.

Women, too, Cole argues, can benefit from the exercise of gardening. He continues: 'Gentlewomen if the ground be not too wet, may doe themselves much good by Kneeling upon a Cushion and weeding. And thus both sexes might divert themselves from Idlenesse and evill Company, which often times prove the ruine of many ingenious people. But perhaps they may thinke it a disparagement to the condition they are in; truly none at all, if it were but put in practice: For we see that those fashions which sometimes seem ridiculous, if once taken up by the Gentry ceases to be so.' This last point is well illustrated by the French nation's refusal to eat potatoes until Louis XVI was persuaded by the agronomist and military pharmacist Antoine Parmentier to grow a crop at Neuilly. As the crop reached harvest time, Louis, having sported a potato flower in his hat, placed an armed guard around the field until the potatoes were safely gathered in. Potatoes took on celebrity status overnight.

Jane Loudon too sees no reason why ladies should not dig, and benefit from it. In *Gardening for Ladies* (1840) she writes:

A lady, with a small light spade may, by repeatedly digging over the same line, and taking out only a little earth at a time, succeed in doing all the digging that can be required in a small garden; and she will not only have the satisfaction of seeing the garden created, as it were, by her own hands, but she will find her health and spirits wonderfully improved by the exercise, and by the reviving smell of the fresh earth. Whatever doubts may be entertained as to the practicability of a lady attending to the culture of culinary vegetables and fruit trees, none can exist respecting her management of the flower garden. That is pre-eminently a woman's department. The culture of flowers implies the lightest possible kind of garden labour...

Cole concludes: 'By this time I hope you will thinke it no dishonour to follow the steps of our Grandsire Adam, who is commonly pictured with a Spade in his hand, to march through the Quarters of your Gardens with the like Instrument, and there to rectifie all the disorders thereof ... So that this Art, with the rest, being improved may bring forth much glory to God, much Honour to the Nation and much Pleasure and Profit to those that delight in it.'

That pleasure Edward Thomas (1878–1917) demonstrates in these lines from 'Digging':

To-day I think
Only with scents, – scents dead leaves yield,
And bracken, and wild carrot's seed,
And the square mustard field;
Odours that rise
When the spade wounds the root of tree,
Rose, currant, raspberry, or goutweed,
Rhubarb or celery;
The smoke's smell, too,
Flowing from where a bonfire burns
The dead, the waste, the dangerous,
And all to sweetness turns.

Weeding

When I have had a busy day, I read what all these experts say,
And often wonder, entre nous, if I could be an expert, too.
I think it must be rather nice to live by giving good advice,
To talk of what the garden needs, instead of pulling up the weeds.

Reginald Arkell (1882–1954)

THE PERILS OF WEEDING

I scarcely dare trust myself to speak of the weeds. They grow as if the devil was in them. I know a lady, a member of the church, and a very good sort of woman, considering the subject condition of that class, who says that the weeds work on her to that extent, that, in going through her garden, she has the greatest difficulty in keeping the ten commandments in anything like an unfractured condition. I asked her which one, but she said, all of them: one felt like breaking the whole lot.

Had C.D. Warner and his parishioner, whom he describes in *My Summer in a Garden* (1918), heard that a weed is a plant in the wrong place, they might have learned to love either the weeds or the act of weeding – as Warner's contemporary Mrs C.W. Earle did, writing in *Pot-Pourri from a Surrey Garden*: 'Weeding! What it means to us all! The worry of seeing the weeds, the labour of taking them up, the way they flourish at busy times, and the dangers that come from zeal without knowledge! Weeding, if tiring, is also a fascinating employment.'

Traditionally women were employed to weed along with boys, but the boys were better paid. Records for an estate in Rotherhithe in 1358 show Alan Gardiner earning 5d. a day, William Devenyssh 4d., Robert Coventre 3d. and nameless women weeders 2½d. a day. In July 1516 weeders in the orchard at Hampton Court Palace were earning only a halfpenny more. The wages of Agnes March, Alice and Elizabeth Alen, Elizabeth Anmun, Joan Smeton, Annes Lewes, Jone Abraham, Margaret Cookstole, Katherine Wite and Agnes Norton were three pence a day, for clearing the ground of charlock, cockles, convolvulus, dodder, thistles, nettles, docks, dandelions and groundsel.

Any experienced gardener will sympathize with the sentiments of William Lawson, who in *A New Orchard and Garden* (1618) writes: '… there will ever be something to do. Weeds are always growing; the great Mother of all living creatures is full of seed in her bowels, and any stirring gives them heat of sun, and being laid near day, they grow.' Modern research has shown that there are advantages to digging weedy patches at night, as just a split-second exposure to daylight triggers seeds in the soil into germination. In Northamptonshire they moan 'One year's seed, seven years' weed' and similarly in Oxfordshire 'One year's seeding makes seven years' weeding', both sayings referring to the fact that if you do fail to remove annual weeds such as shepherd's purse and chickweed before they produce seed, you will face many more of them, as their seeds germinate easily and some of them produce several generations in one season.

WHEN TO WEED

Moist soil is best for weeding and dry for hoeing. As Hill says in *The Gardener's Labyrinth* (1577): 'Here remember, that you never take in hand or begin the weeding of your beds, before the earth be made soft, through the store of rain falling a day or two before.' He also says: '… for occasion will move the carefull Gardener to weed dainty hearbs, being yet young and tender, lest grosse weeds in the growing up with them, may annoy and hinder their increasing.'

J.C. Loudon offers sound advice on both weeding and general maintenance in his *Encyclopaedia of Gardening* (1822):

In passing to and from your work, or, on any occasion, through any part of what is considered under the charge of the gardener, keep a vigilant look-out for weeds, decayed leaves, or any other deformity, and remove them, or some of them, in passing along. Attend to this particularly on walks, edgings and in passing through hot-houses etc. In like manner, take off insects, or leaves infected by them. Much in large as well as in small gardens may be effected by this sort of timely or preventive attention, which induces suitable habits for a young gardener, and occupies very little time.

By following Cobbett's advice in *The English Gardener* – 'In the spring, March or early in April, move the tops of the beds with a fork, and carefully pick out all weeds that make their appearance' – you can make the beds look tidy. That is the time too to get out perennial weeds such as bindweed and ground elder before they make a march. Use a small long-handled fork, but remember that in doing it you may expose dormant seeds.

In her guide for April in *The Amateur Gardener* Jane Loudon advises: 'Weeds will put in strong claims to be considered spring flowering plants if not looked after at this season, and if allowed to reach this stage they will deposit as much seed as will suffice to crop the garden for the summer.' For May, she says: 'Weeds are now full of vigour, and will soon shoot up to a surprising size if not dealt with in time. Apart from the advantages of cleanliness to the produce, it is always a pleasure to see luxuriant crops of vegetables quite free from weeds.'

ABOVE *A hoe for every task: four to draw (left) and three to thrust (left).*

Tusser too earmarks May for the battle against weeds in *Five Hundred Points of Good Husbandry* (1573):

> From Maie til October leave cropping, for why? …
> To weeding away, as soone as yee may,
> Now sets doe crave some weeding to have …
> In Maie get a weede hooke, a crotch and a glove,
> And weed out such weedes …

HOW TO WEED

In *Children's Gardens* (1907), the Hon. Mrs Evelyn Cecil (aka Alicia Amherst) writes:

> Enjoy the spring, children, to the full, for it is indeed a lovely time, and like your own childhood, should be full of promise, and fresh, gay, happy innocence. But with new life comes new work … and business must start in real earnest now. It is not only pretty trees and flowers that begin to grow, but the revival comes to weeds as well, and very soon they would choke and kill the more tender plants; so the first duty in spring is to weed. There is a right and a wrong way of doing everything, and often a strange instinct inclines the choice to the wrong. Even in weeding this may be the case. A badly weeded garden may look quite nice and tidy for a few days, but if the weeds have not been carefully and completely pulled up by the roots and taken away, they will soon be as bad as ever again. Breaking off the tops will not do … Some things, like groundsel, which you very likely bring into the house for your canary birds, are easy to pull up. Oh how I have tugged and pulled at the twisted roots of nettle in my wild garden, following the stringy yellow fibres a yard or more along the ground; or worse still have been my struggles with 'ground elder' which made its way everywhere. It was a yearly toil, but at last I conquered, and made the weeds understand that although wild, yet it was a flower and not a 'bear garden'.

C.D. Warner as usual turns weeding into a moral quest:

> I believe I have found, if not original sin, at least vegetable total depravity in my garden; and it was there before I went into it. It is the

bunch, or joint, or snake grass – whatever it is called. As I do not know the names of all the weeds and plants, I have to do as Adam did in his garden – name things as I find them. This grass has a slender beautiful stalk, and when you cut it down or pull up a long root of it, you fancy it is got rid of; but in a day or two it will come up in the same spot in half a dozen vigorous blades. Cutting down and pulling up is what it thrives on. Extermination rather helps it. If you follow a slender white root, it will be found to run under the ground until it meets another slender white root; and you will soon unearth a network of them, with a knot somewhere, sending out dozens of sharp-pointed, healthy shoots, every joint prepared to be an independent life and plant. The only way to deal with it is to take one part hoe and two parts fingers, and carefully dig it out, not leaving a joint anywhere. It will take a little time, say all summer to dig out thoroughly a small patch; but if you once dig it out, and keep it out, you will have no further trouble.

I have said it was total depravity. Here it is. If you attempt to pull up and root out any sin in you, which shows on the surface – if it does not show you do not care for it – you may have noticed how it runs into an interior network of sins, and an ever-sprouting branch of them roots somewhere; and that you cannot pull out one without making a general internal disturbance, and rooting up your whole being. I suppose it is less trouble to quietly cut them off at the top – say once a week, on Sunday, when you put on your religious clothes and face – so that no one will see them, and to try to eradicate the network within … The weeds … have hateful moral qualities. To cut down a weed is, therefore, to do a moral action. I feel as if I were destroying sin. My hoe becomes an instrument of retributive justice. I am an apostle of Nature. This view of the matter lends a dignity to the act of hoeing which … lifts it into the regions of ethics. Hoeing becomes not a pastime but a duty. And you get to regard it so as the days and the weeds lengthen.

If you are digging out pernicious weeds from a small patch as C.D. Warner suggests, leaving the area blank for a season, you might try Jekyll's pretty idea, which she describes in an article published in 1937: 'There is not always in a garden an opportunity for having special borders for annuals, yet such a chance occurs from time to time, and especially when ground is

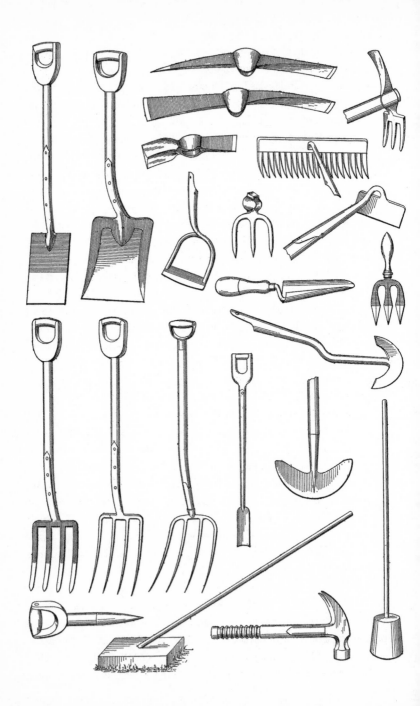

being slowly restored from unavoidable neglect, or when there are regions infested with Couch or some other troublesome weed, such as cannot be entirely got rid of by one forking over. Here is the opportunity for the bed of annuals, to be used as what gardeners call a cleaning crop.' Catch-crop salads would be an alternative.

Hill cautions against arming yourself with weapons for aggressive weeding: 'In this plucking up, and purging of the Garden beds of weeds and stones, the same about the plants ought rather to be exercised with the hand, than with an Iron instrument, for feare of feebling the young plants, yet small and tender of growth.' It is so easy to let a hoe slip and decapitate a favourite plant.

Old steel knives whose ends have broken off are excellent for extracting weeds lodged in between paving slabs or in lawns, as Kipling recalls in his wry lines in 'The Glory of the Garden' of 1911 in which he describes 'better men than we' who:

> ... go out and start their working lives
> At grubbing weeds from gravel paths with broken dinner knives.

It is also easy to pull out plants as well as weeds, especially as weeds are past masters at disguise, inveigling themselves by mixing with similar-leaved or -stemmed plants – bindweed twining through *Viola cornuta*, for example – as the parable of the wheat and the tares (described in the Gospel of St Matthew) demonstrates. 'The kingdom of heaven is likened unto a man which sowed good seed in his field: But while men slept, his enemy came and sowed tares among the wheat, and went his way. But when the blade was sprung up, and brought forth fruit, then appeared the tares also ... the householder ... said ... An enemy hath done this. The servants said unto him, Wilt thou then that we go and gather them up? But he said, Nay; lest while ye gather up the tares, ye root up also the wheat with them.' The tares were mistranslated and are actually darnel, which requires an expert eye to discern in its early stages. What is more, darnel is a host to the fungal disease ergot, so it is a doubly pernicious weed.

Caroline Hamilton, in *The Garden Notebook* she kept from 1827 to 1846, believes winged visitors to the garden will help: 'Birds should be

LEFT *Plenty of tools to sharpen, many of them multipurpose.*

encouraged rather than destroyed in a garden, provided that the fruits are protected by nets, and cherry trees. They pick up not only caterpillars but the seeds of weeds.'

WEEDING WEAR

J.C. and Jane Loudon write copiously on weeding, suggesting that doing it little and often is a good guide. They also advise on what to wear. Urging readers of *The Villa Gardener* (1850) to 'attend to personal habits and cleanliness', J.C. Loudon takes, as always, a paternalistic tone: 'Never perform any operation without gloves on your hands that you can do with gloves on; even weeding is far more effectually and expeditiously performed by gloves, the fore-fingers and thumbs of which terminate in wedge-like thimbles of steel, kept sharp. Most other operations may be performed with common gloves. Thus, no gardener need have hands like bears' paws.' When my washing-up gloves start to leak I give them a second airing for weeding.

Jane Loudon also recommends gloves *The Ladies Companion to the Flower Garden* (1840): 'The lady … should also have a pair of stiff thick leather gloves, or gauntlets, to protect her hands … from the stones, weeds, etc., which she turns over with the earth, and which ought to be picked out and thrown into a small light wheelbarrow, which may be easily moved from place to place.'

Her husband also says: 'Let your dress be clean, neat, simple and harmonious in form and colour: in your movements maintain an erect posture, easy and free gait and motion; let your manner be respectful and decorous to your superiors; and conduct fair and agreeable to your equals.' He appears not to take account of the need to bend, crawl and kneel to hand weed. Assuming his weeding readers to be paid workers, he adds:

> Elevate, ameliorate, and otherwise improve, any raw, crude, harsh or inharmonious features in your physiognomy, by looking often at the faces of agreeable people, by occupying your mind with agreeable and useful ideas, and by continually instructing yourself by reading. This will also give you features if you have none. Remember that you are paid and maintained by and for the use of and pleasure of your employer, who may no more wish to see a dirty, ragged, uncouth-looking, grinning, or conceited biped in his garden, than a starved, haggard, untutored horse in his stable.

DANDELIONS AND OTHER FELONS

You could always try eating your weeds. Ground elder is also known as goutweed, for good reason, and up until June it is a delicious spinach substitute. Nettles, which were introduced by the Romans, became a traditional savoury spring pudding. The Reverend Hilderic Friend includes the following nugget on nettles in *Flowers and Flower Lore* (1886): 'We are probably all familiar with the saying "Grasp your nettle!" ... If one can only summon courage enough to seize the Nettle-leaf firmly, and squeeze it hard between the fingers, it gives no pain, the spikes being crushed and broken without piercing the skin.' If it does sting, the antidote, dock – as difficult to eradicate – is normally near by. He also tells us that 'At Hitchin in Hertfordshire, the people used to express their feelings towards their neighbours by decorating their doors before morning ... those who were not liked having the fact indicated by the presence of Nettles ...'

Dandelions are very rich in potash and are an excellent diuretic – hence their old name of piss-a-bed. A lunchtime salad of the leaves in spring cleanses the system wonderfully. However, as once they have flowered they send their myriad feathery seeds all over the garden you may wish to remove them sooner rather than later.

Apart from the threat of thistledown before weeding them out remember the old Suffolk saying, 'Cut your thistles before St John, You will have two instead of one.' St John's Day is 24 June.

Some ornamental plants can turn out to be thugs. Miller describes one example in his *Gardener's Dictionary* (1731): 'Persicaria ... being Plants of no Use at present ... a very sharp acrid Plant, from whence it had its Name of Arse smart ... is a very bad Weed, if once it gets Possession in a Garden; for the Roots extend themselves greatly under-ground, and arise from every Joint (as doth Couch grass), so that it is with great Difficulty extirpated.' Persicaria is a member of the *Polygonaceae* family, and therefore a relative of Japanese knotweed, which is classed as a pernicious weed.

Three hundred years later in *Garden Wisdom* Marion Cran warns about another: 'Of Petasites fragrans one must give serious warning. It has its loveliness, and is what one may truly call a most amiable weed; yet weed it is on the grandest scale ... it travels far, is almost impossible to eradicate, and is something to fear when it gets hold of a garden.'

Tools

He that would perfect his work must first sharpen his tools.

Confucius (*c.* 551–479 BC)

THE GARDENER'S ALLIES

Our hands are our original tools, but man has long used gardening implements. The Museum of Garden History in London has antlers that men used for drawing soil in ancient times. In the 1190s Alexander Neckham wrote in *De Utensilibus* (Concerning Tools) on how to equip the gardener: 'Let him also have stakes and sticks, well-tried and hardened in the fire. Let him also have a two-sided billhook for tearing out brambles, thorns, prickly plants and butchers' broom … and mattocks to rip out undergrowth, weeds, nettles … thistles … These are also easily pulled out with a hooked grub-axe.' Some of these are still essential tools for anyone clearing ground for a new garden.

According to Tusser in *Five Hundred Points of Good Husbandry* (1573):

Strong and silent: gardeners at Rhyddings Park on 16 October 1909.

Through cunning with dible, rake, mattock, and spade,
by line and by leavell, trim garden is made.

Dibble, rake and spade remain our essential garden tools; today the mattock has been replaced by the garden fork.

Thomas Carlyle found a sickle useful at his garden at 5 Cheyne Row, Chelsea. In 1840 he wrote to his brother Alick: '[I want] to tell you what good I have got of the axe and sickle you sent me long since ... The sickle hangs on a branch of our old scrag of a cherry tree (which grows large quantities of cherries, mostly eaten by sparrows); I mow the grass with it, hew down the superfluous vine-branches.' It was commonplace to leave your sickle in a garden tree so that it was near to hand for any odd job.

John Evelyn devotes several pages to drawings of garden tools and implements in *Elysium Brittanicum* (written *c.* 1659 but not published during his lifetime). He recommends upmarket rollers for rolling 'gravel walkes' – a job that, like rolling lawns, in his time was left to the gardener: '... the best are made of the hardest Marble ... procured from the ruines of many places in Smyrna when old Colomns of demolish'd Antiquities are being sawd off towards the vino of the pedistall and at the part of modell where the shaft deminishes makes excelent rollers ... may be procur'd by the friendship of some Merchant trading into the Levant.' Other tools he mentions include moletraps, water barrels, pruning knives, spades, a four-poster bed with net curtains to 'draw over and preserve the Choysest flowers', various wheeled carts and much more.

Carts were an essential feature of the garden, as was the more wieldy wheelbarrow, the earliest depiction of which is on a medieval wall in Norfolk. Beeton describes the wheelbarrow as 'A box open at the top, supported by two legs, and in front by a wheel, which may be driven forward when the legs are lifted off the ground by means of the handles that project from the hinder part of the barrow, and which usually form part of the framework on which the body or box is supported' – a description which, if you did not already know what a wheelbarrow looked like, might leave you no wiser.

Once again the advice Jane Loudon gives in *The Ladies Companion to the Flower Garden* (1840) is relevant to any gardener, male or female. She says: 'A wheelbarrow is a necessary appendage to every garden; and one intended for the use of a lady ought to be made as light as possible, and the handles curved so as to require very little stooping. The wheel also ought to be made broad, to prevent it from injuring the walk. In addition to the wheelbarrow, there may be a hand-barrow, consisting of a square basket with two long poles, so as to be carried between two persons.'

Thomas Jefferson appears to have done a time-and-motion study on the efficiency of using a wheelbarrow. In the *Garden and Farm Books* he kept for his three Virginian estates, he writes: 'The greatest service which can be rendered any country is to add a useful plan Julius Shard fills the two-wheeled barrow in 3 minutes, and carries it 30 yards in 1½ minutes, more. Now this 4 loads of the common barrow with one wheel. So that suppose the 4 loads put in at the same time viz. 3 minutes, 4 trips will take 4 x 1½ minutes = 6, which added to three minutes = 9 minutes to fill and carry the same earth which was filled and carried in the two-wheeled barrow in 4½.' Poor Julius Shard!

Writers sometimes mention tools that we no longer use today. Fitzherbert, for instance, describes in his *Book of Husbandry* of 1534 something that sounds like a daisy or dandelion grubber, which would give the gardener the purchase to lift the roots of these plants effortlessly out of the ground: 'Then must ye have a wedynge-hoke with a socket, set upon a little staffe a yard longe, and this hoke wolde be grounde sharpe, both behind and before. In his other hand he hath a forked stycke a yarde longe, and with his forked stycke he putteth the weed from him, and he putteth the hoke beyond the root of the wede, and putteth it to him, and cutteth the weed fast by the earth.'

Beeton describes something similar, which he calls a daisy fork, in his *New Dictionary of Every-day Gardening*:

Daisies should never be allowed to flower: a good daisy rake, with a little trouble, will remove all flowers as they come out; but the only plan to clear a lawn effectually of these disagreeable weeds is to take them out with the daisy fork wherever they are found. This handy little tool is made in different forms, or rather with handles of different lengths, but the principle is the same in all … This fork is thrust into the ground, so as to take the daisy plant between the prongs or tines. The iron ring which is attached to the iron is then pressed against the ground and acts as a fulcrum, on which the cleft end is raised when the handle is pressed downwards. The raising of the cleft end lifts the daisy out of the ground. It is sometimes used to remove docks and dandelions … Daisies, and indeed all weeds, are more easily removed in wet weather, or after a shower.

He goes on to explain how to make your own daisy rake:

A daisy rake is very easily made … First of all a thin plate of iron is obtained, and cut into broad teeth along one edge: the iron should be just so thick as not to bend easily to pressure or any resistance. Two slips of ash are then cut out, each being of the length of the iron, and about five eighths inch in thickness and 2 inches wide. These are bevelled towards the inner edge – the upper one but slightly, and the other to thickness of ¼ inch. The iron is placed between them, and the two pieces of wood and the iron are firmly fastened together by stout screws or rivets. A handle is then put into the rake … Holes should be drilled through the iron plate to admit of the passage of the rivets and handle. The teeth of the rake should be slightly bent upwards, or, in other words, slightly curved.

Did anyone actually make this rake, or is this description armchair garden writing gone mad?

Leverage to eradicate daisies and a turf spade for professionals.

Pruning

THE CUTTING EDGE

Cutting tidies and regenerates plants, whether grass, trees, shrubs or perennials. But as the Reverend Henry Burgess wrote in *The Amateur Gardener's Year-Book* (1854), 'Every advancing bud which is cut off is so much abstracted from those which remain, and life thus wasted ought to have been concentrated in the tree'. Pruners should find a balance: pruning allows more light and less competition, but takes away leaves that are essential for photosynthesis. Before the invention of secateurs, a variety of pruning knives were used and they remained the head gardener's favourite until the second half of the twentieth century.

The Dundee-born scientist Patrick Blair wrote in *The Botanick Essays*, published in 1720: 'The lateral tendency of the sap when interrupted in its ascent, analogous to that of the blood at an amputation, is obvious from an experiment of Mr. Fairchild's … He observes that if a tree is planted in the autumn it ought not to be topped until the spring following, for the sap circulates more agreeably when allowed to ascend directly to the top of the autumnal shrub than when interrupted by cutting it off at the planting.' Today many tree and shrub experts advise autumn planting so that the plant starts to establish in cooler and wetter weather, then a good prune before the drying spring winds damage new leaves.

George Glenny in his *The Gardener's Every-Day Book containing Plain Instructions for the Cultivation of all Classes of Flowers, Fruit and Vegetables, and the Practical Management of Every Department of Horticulture and Floriculture* of 1863 advises: 'June: As a general rule, without specifying every individual tree or shrub, all of them can be improved in form by the judicious use of the knife before they make their growth, because afterwards we are restrained by the bloom buds.' However, most shrubs are best pruned after flowering which, with the range of shrubs we have, can mean almost any month of the year, although it is not advisable to prune in the coldest months of winter.

CLIPPED PLANTS AND TOPIARY

Gardeners have clipped plants into interesting shapes for centuries. Nearly 400 years ago William Lawson suggested in *A New Orchard and Garden* (1618): 'Your gardener can frame your lesser wood to the shape of men

armed in the field, ready to give battell: or swift-running Grey Hounds to chase the Deere, or hunt the Hare. This kind of hunting shall not waste your corne, nor much your coyne.'

Celia Fiennes, who trotted around late Stuart England visiting houses and gardens, notes in her *Great Journey* of 1698 (a journal which incidentally remained unread until the poet Southey found it and quoted it in 1812): 'I went to Banstead where the parson ... has diverted himself in his garden these fifty yeares ... has curious hedges, one Garden with grass plotts and earth walks, cut and wedd, his grass plotts has stones of divers formes and sizes, which he names Gods and Goddesses, and hedges and arbours of thorn soe neatly cut and in all figures in great rounds.'

The Edwardians Mrs C.W. Earle and Miss Ethel Case also noticed unusually clipped plants while travelling together. In *Pot-Pourri by Two* she writes: 'I saw a Choisya ternata today trained up a high wall and very much pruned in: true, the flowers were mostly at the top but it made a good covering for a bare wall in a way that I have never seen before.'

Gardeners wishing to try their hands at topiary can find sensible and practical advice in the pages of the *Book of Topiary* by Charles H. Curtis and W. Gibson, of 1904.

The work of clipping Topiary trees is not so difficult as might be expected. There are several points that should always be remembered. Symmetry and shape are necessary to make a good tree; and this may be said to be the first and most important factor in the work. Another point is to take particular care that the shears do not cut off more than

ABOVE *The boater adds an air of elegance ... in winter?*

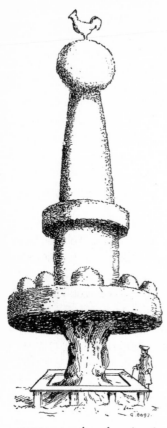

is necessary. By that I mean, never to allow the shears to cut deep enough into the tree to make a hole. Another very important point to aim at is to give the tree as smooth and even an appearance as possible after the work is finished. I am perfectly aware that, in a large collection of yews or other clipped trees, there are always some that it is impossible to clip properly, on account of weak growth, or some other cause. For instance, trees that are growing in a part of the garden where they are fully exposed to wind and storm are almost certain to get into an unhealthy condition. The growth becomes weak and stunted, or perhaps the branches get worked out of place, or even die out altogether. In the case of trees of that description, no matter how much tying is done or how carefully they are clipped, they can never be made to have the same appearance as those that are full of young growth and are in a healthy and vigorous state.

Unless you have exceptional abilities, you will gain confidence and skill using lines and guidance markers when clipping. Today's revival of interest in topiary has led to the availability of a large choice of shapes and formers, large and small, simple and intricate.

Lines are particularly useful for straight hedges, as Curtis and Gibson explain:

Perhaps of all the different kind of shapes there are to clip in the Topiary garden, hedges require the most skill and care, and only the

ABOVE: *The Harlington Yew, as clipped 1729–90.*

most experienced men should be allowed to undertake the work of clipping them. Hedges in the garden are mostly planted in such a way that their entire length is visible, and of course the most casual observer can see at a glance whether they are properly clipped or if there are any shear marks visible on them. If the hedge is composed mostly of curves, then of course the clipping is not such a difficult matter. A long, straight hedge and one that is almost entirely made up of curves, differ in the same respect with regard to the ease with which they can be clipped, exactly in the same way as a round or an oval tree. When clipping a straight hedge a person should never trust entirely to the eye, and lines should always be used; and for the purpose nothing is better than ordinary garden lines ...

In the case of hedges that are cut into battlements at the top, these should have a line stretched lengthways along the ground, another along the base of the battlements, and another along the top of the battlements; and whatever size and width the battlements are, say, for instance, two feet high and two feet in width between them, a stick cut exactly two feet in length or a two-foot rule should be used to measure the exact height and distance between the battlements; and if those precautions are taken, any person with a fair knowledge of the art of clipping can hardly with ordinary care and attention get wrong; as, after all, the work of clipping Topiary trees is not so difficult as might be expected.

You will also need, of course, a good platform to work from. Again these have recently been introduced to the amateur market.

The poet, essayist and literary critic Alexander Pope used his wit to rail against the extremes of topiary in the *Guardian* in 1713: 'For the benefit of all my loving Country-men of this curious Taste, I shall here publish a Catalogue of Greens to be disposed of by an eminent Town-Gardiner ... Any Ladies that please may have their own Effigies in Myrtle, or their Husbands in Horn beam.'

Today's gardeners should go forth and sift the humour from the humus and clip new shoots into pleasing tips.

Select bibliography

For titles for which several editions were published, I have given the date of first publication in brackets and the date of any other editions I used.

Amherst, The Hon. Alicia, *A History of Gardening in England*, Quaritch 1895

Anon. (illustrated by M.W.G. Wilson), *Memories*, T.N. Foulis, reprinted 1918

Austen, Ralph, *A Treatise of Fruit Trees Together with The Spirituall Use of an Orchard*, 1653

Baron, Robert C. (ed.), *The Garden and Farm Books of Thomas Jefferson*, Fulcrum, 1987

Beeton, S., *Beeton's New Dictionary of Every-day Gardening*, Ward, Lock & Co. Ltd, 1862

—, *Beeton's Gardening Book*, Ward, Lock & Co. Ltd.

—, *Beeton's Shilling Gardening Book*, Ward, Lock & Co. Ltd.

Bewick, Thomas, *A General History of Quadrapeds* (1790), 3rd edition 1792

Blomfield, Reginald, *The Formal Garden in England* (1892), Macmillan and Co., 3rd edition 1901

Bright, Henry A., *A Year in a Lancashire Garden*, Macmillan and Co., 1901

Burbidge, F.W., *The Book of the Scented Garden*, The Bodley Head, 1905

Cobbett, William, *Cottage Economy*, A New Edition, London 1823

—, *The English Gardener* (1829), London 1833

Cran, Marion, *Garden Wisdom from the writings of Marion Cran 1910–41*, Herbert Jenkins

Culpeper, Nicholas, *The English Physitian* (Culpeper's *Herbal*), 1651

—, *A Directory for Midwives*, 1651 (Culpeper's *Book of Birth*, 1985)

Dallimore, W. *Holly, Yew and Box*, John Lane, 1908

Dixon Hunt, John and Willis, Peter (eds), *The Genius of the Place: The English Landscape Garden 1620–1820*, Elek, 1975

Downing, A.J., *Cottage Residences*, 1842

Earle, Mrs. C.W., *Pot-Pourri from a Surrey Garden*, Nelson, 1918

Earle, Mrs. C.W. et al, *Garden Colour*, J.M. Dent, 1905

Friend, Revd Hilderic, *Flowers and Flower Lore*, 3rd edition, Swan Sonnenschein, 1886

Gerard, John, *The Herball or Generall Historie of Plantes* (1597), Very much Enlarged and Amended by Thomas Johnson, Citizen and Apothecarye, 1636

Grieve, Maude, *A Modern Herbal*, 1931

Harvey, John, *Medieval Gardens*, Batsford, 1981 (many of the medieval quotations have been taken from this invaluable, scholarly and comprehensive book)

Hibberd, Shirley, *Rustic Adornments for Homes of Taste*, 1856

Hill, Thomas, *The Gardener's Labyrinth*, 1577 (ed. Richard Mabey, Oxford University Press, 1987)

Hole, S. Reynolds (Dean of Rochester), *Our Gardens*, J.M. Dent & Co., 1899

—, *A Book About Roses: How to grow and show them*, Nelson, 1901

Holland, Philemon, *The History of the World commonly called The Natural History of C. Plinius Secundus*, edited by Paul Turner, Centaur Press, 1962

Huxley, Anthony, *An Illustrated History of Gardening*, Paddington Press, 1978

— (editor in chief), *The New Royal Horticultural Society Dictionary of Gardening*, vols. 1–4, The Stockton Press, 1992

Jekyll, Gertrude, *Wood and Garden*, Longmans & Co., 1899

—, *Home and Garden*, Longmans & Co., 1900

—, *Roses for English Gardens*, Country Life Library, 1902

—, *Colour in the Flower Garden*, 1908 (after 3rd edition *Colour Schemes for the Flower Garden*, 1914)

—, *Children and Gardens*, Country Life Library, 1908

—, *Gardens for Small Country Houses*, Country Life Library, 1912

—, *A Gardener's Testament*, Country Life Library, 1937

Lawson, William, *A New Orchard and Garden*, 1618

—, *The Country House-Wifes Garden*, 1623

Leapman, Michael, *The Ingenious Mr Fairchild*, Headline, 2000

Lipscomb, Andrew A. and Bergh, Albert Ellery (eds), *The Writings of Thomas Jefferson*, 1903–4

Loudon, Mrs Jane, *The Ladies Companion to The Flower Garden* (1840) William Smith, 4th edition 1846

—, *The Amateur Gardener* (1847), revised and edited by W. Robinson, Frederick Warne and Co, 1880

Loudon, John Claudius, *The Villa Garden* (1850), 2nd edition 1850

Miller, Philip, *The Gardener's Dictionary in Three Volumes* (1731), 3rd edition 1748

Mitford, Mary R., *Our Village*, Macmillan and Co., 1910

Molyneux, Edwin, *Chrysanthemums and their Culture*, London 1888

Palladius, *Palladius on Husbandry*, trans. B. Lodge, London 1873

Rivers, Thomas, *The Miniature Fruit Garden* (1850), Longmans, Green, Reader and Dyer, sixteenth edition 1870

Robinson, William, *The English Flower Garden* (1883), fifteenth edition 1933

—, *The Vegetable Garden*, John Murray, 1905

Sinclair Rohde, Eleanour, *Herbs and Herb Gardening*, Medici, 1936, reprinted 1946

—, *Oxford's College Gardens*, Herbert Jenkins, 1932

Suttons & Sons, Reading, *The Culture of Vegetables and Flowers from Seeds and Roots* (1913), Simpkin Marshall Ltd, eighteenth edition 1930

The Fruit and Vegetable Finder, fifth edition 1995, from the Heritage Seed Library of the Henry Doubleday Research Association (HDRA) and the National Fruit Collection at Brogdale

Thompson, Robert, *The Gardener's Assistant* (1880), New Edition in 6 Volumes, The Gresham Publishing Company, 1900

Thomson, David, *Handy Book of The Flower-Garden*, William Blackwood and Sons, 1868

Tusser, Thomas, *Five Hundred Points of Good Husbandry* (1573), revised editions 1580, 1878 and 1931 (Oxford University Press, 1984)

Index